From the Cotton Field to Capitol Hill

Shirley Noel Adkins

Copyright © 2021 Shirley Noel Adkins
All rights reserved
First Edition

PAGE PUBLISHING, INC.
Conneaut Lake, PA

First originally published by Page Publishing 2021

ISBN 978-1-64628-773-4 (pbk)
ISBN 978-1-64628-774-1 (digital)

Printed in the United States of America

Dedication

I dedicate this journey to Ester Lee Stanback (Mutt Dear), Amie Adams (Big Mama), who were alma maters from the school of mother wit. A college degree doesn't compare to what you taught to me and my siblings, William Edd, Reola, Osieola, Amie. I received my degree from the "University of Mother Wit" in our three-room house. From earth to heaven, I extend my appreciation, respect, and love to you both. I am so grateful for your teachings and the morals, values, principles, and standards you instilled in me to become the person I am today and achieve whatever is put before me. Love you much forever.

To my son, Jerry Sr.; my daughter-in-law, Catrina; my grandchildren Jerrika, LeDre, and Jerry Jr.; my grandson-in-law, Holly; great-grands, Braylan and Kerry, KJ and Paityn: Granny, love you.

To my sister's friend, Jacqueline Clemmons, thank you for your prayers, for pushing and giving me a deadline to complete this assignment.

Jacqueline James, thank you for your love and encouragement and walking with me through many of my adult spiritual moments.

Lucy, I appreciate you being by my side through all my Capitol Hill moments.

Francis Vaughn, thank you for being that go-to person in our family. Love you beyond measure, cousin.

Since beginning my stories from the cotton field to Capitol Hill, my brother, William (Poochie) Noel, my cousin, Barbara Ford, and my father, William Perkins, have transitioned this life. From earth to heaven, You are forever loved.

Table of Contents

Preface 7
Chapter 1: Growing up in the South 9
        Three-Room House 14
        Big Mama Passing 24
        Picking Cotton 26
        Racist Experiences as a Teenager 32
        County School Counselor 32
        Corner Store 38
        Rosa Park Experience 41
        Senior Year Expulsion: 43
        Mutt Dear Response To School Expulsion 45
        State Fair 47
        Being Shot At 48
Chapter 2: Adulthood 52
        Marriage 54
        Biological Father 59
        Call Into Ministry 68
        Initial Sermon 77
        Living Abroad 79
        Transitioning Back To The U.S. 88
        Being Homeless 92
Chapter 3: Capitol Hill 101
        Applying For A Loan 107

Senator Harry Reid 114
Senator Rockefeller 118
Meeting Senator Obama 130

Preface

Of the seventeen states known for producing cotton, Alabama ranks number 7. As a small child growing up in rural Lauderdale County, Alabama, I saw during the summer months fields sparkling with cotton so white it made you want to run through the rows of them and grab hold of their softness. I thought it was the most beautiful thing anyone could look at. It seldom snows in Alabama, so when I looked across the fields, cotton in my young mind was an image of snow. This image soon left me when I began to pick cotton from those fields at harvesttime during the summer. It was the hottest months of the year. The sun beamed down, and the heat baked your skin, as you bent your back over from sunup to sundown with a cotton sack over your shoulder, dragging up and down the rows of cotton that seemed endless. If cotton wasn't picked a particular way from its stems, you could sustain an injury that would hinder your work because of pain. If not done properly, pulling cotton out of boll that held it in place on the stalks could wound your finger and scratch and scar your arms. The image of snow soon left me because snow is cold and wet but this was hot, miserable, and irritating. My imagination soon turned to a different direction when I was physically put into the position of having to pick the beautiful snow-like cotton. This type of work today would have been considered as slavery—cruel, abusive, and punishing.

Thank God those days of working no longer exist. Being a child, I didn't know how long I would have to do this type of work. As I grew older, I realized that my imagination was a vision of how to get out of what I was doing and move into bigger and greater things. This is what my book is about: how we can turn our imagination, fantasies, dreams, and visions real; how we can go through life and end up in success; and how we should walk in the call and purpose we were created for. How we walk through our cotton-field experiences determines our strength, growth, and walk toward life's purpose.

We all have cotton-field experiences. Your cotton field may not look like mine, but if you have been in a place or position where you told yourself that there has to be a better way or if you wanted something different in life, then you've had a cotton-field experience. Things look good from afar until you're directly in it. Once there, you see that what looked good from a distance isn't good up close. It may sound cliché, but the grass is not always greener on the other side. How you got there is hindsight, but how you get out answers and tells about who you are and what you're made of. You never know what you have inside until you're put into a position that makes you go deep within yourself to open your mind and see through the eyes of your heart. The heart speaks volumes to the mind. Allow the mind to receive and act upon what is being spoken. It's not the easiest thing to do, but the process is rewarding when you get there and look at the journey you took. Walk with me through my journey from the cotton fields to Capitol Hill.

Chapter One
Growing up in the South

Growing up in the South had its challenges. I realized very early that no matter where you live in this world, there are challenges. After racial segregation, things changed. I discovered that negativity and racism follow you. It makes no difference what you do and what laws are in place. Things remain the same. How you respond to what comes your way makes you a winner or a loser. Life experiences will either make you or break you. Life is full of ups and downs, and how we handle and overcome those challenges answers and says who you are and what you are made of. As long as there is life in our bodies, we continue to learn. The day we stop learning is the day of our demise.

Life experiences and challenges are our atlas. They direct the path we must follow to reach our goals, purpose, and destiny. Life challenges made me who I am and led me on a path that taught me to look further than self and others to reach my purpose and destiny. Many books are written to teach us how to and how not to do things. But are the answers in the books we read, or do the answers lie within oneself?

Many people are still asking the same question I once asked myself. That question for me was what my purpose was in life. Unknown to you, you like myself have the answer. You can't see it because it's too close to you, and all the time, it's staring you in the face. You have the answer, just as I had the answer. The answers are found in our struggles, and your strength is built in the struggles as you journey through challenges and circumstances. The answer to the question I had asked myself for so many years was there all along, but I didn't discover the answer until all the pieces fell into place. This started in the cotton fields. If you are still seeking and asking what your purpose in life is, go back to where your life started.

Alabama is my foundation. My challenges, strength, purpose, tenacity, and maturity were created, established, and designed in this state. I was created and built from the history and reputation of this state. What I experienced and endured strengthened me for life's future challenges. They always say that you are a product of your environment. Think about where you were born, the state and city you were raised in, and the history of that state. Can you identify something within that state that made you who you are today? There is more to your life's purpose that meets the eye based on where you were born.

Everything made is built on a foundation. When a house is built, the only way it can stand firm and sustain whatever comes its way depends on the type of foundation it's built from. Everything newly built is not built firmly and made strong yet. The slightest wind or circumstance can knock it or you over. Life experiences and challenges are just like that. These experiences and challenges build us. How you sustain yourself strengthens the foundation of what you are made of and where you came from. When an obstacle comes, you don't cave in and fall to pieces. You stand. Circumstances of life provide and prove the strength of the anchor and foundation of your character. The next obstacle that comes along will be easier to sustain, and the foundation will be made stronger. We are built, molded, and shaped by life's circumstances. Circumstances don't make us who we are. They reveal who you are.

Everything in life that happens to us is allowed to shape us into the person we were created and designed to be. Nothing happens by chance or coincidence. We all were created with divine design.

I am sharing my story as a witness to how God can turn our struggles into triumphs, our lack into an overflow, our pain into joy, and our weakness into strength. My story is God's glory. Those that know me personally see God's glory but don't know my story.

God's glory is not a secret to be kept to the self; it's to be shared so that others can see how real God is and find strength and comfort knowing that all things works for the good to them who love God and are *called* according to His purpose (Romans 8:28). We are called with purpose, and with that purpose, we are covered for the call. Consistency leads to our purpose, whatever the purpose is. No one is above or without trials and tribulations. I don't know of anyone that lives a life of complete happiness or a life without some obstacle or another. In my story, you may understand why you've gone through some of the things you've gone through or are still going through. And you will live to tell and share them.

Every person in the universe regardless of race, social status, or religious beliefs has two life purposes, and that is to live and to die. The in-betweens in life before death are trials and tribulations—things that make you into the person you are. Everyone experiences them, and no one is exempted.

Alabama is a beautiful state. It is one of the cleanest, most attractive, and most resourceful states I've lived thus far. I have lived in numerous places, and in comparison to some places I have lived, I may be a little biased because Alabama is where I was born and raised, but it is by far the most beautiful place I've lived. As I've grown and matured mentally and spiritually, its beauty surpasses the pain and hurt of its history.

After retiring from the legislative government in 2009 from Washington, DC, I came full circle back. "You can take the girl out the country, but you can't take the country out of the girl" has some truth to it. Thirty-five years of living in other places—and to name a few of those places, Texas, Virginia, Maryland, Washington State, Illinois, the District of Columbia, the United Kingdom—and there is no place like home. Places I have been fortunate to have visited are the Netherlands, Amsterdam, Holland, Scotland, Wales, Ireland, Bath, Belgium, Brussels, Germany, France, London, Oxford, the West Indies, and several states within the United States. No matter where I lived or visited, Alabama always tugged at a corner tucked away in my heart to return.

As beautiful as Alabama is, it still carries negative stereotypes and racial bigotry. The ugly history behind the state lingers in the minds and hearts of many people and rightfully so. Those who have never lived in the state associate the name with the civil rights movement in the sixties with the Montgomery bus boycott, the violence that took place with the Freedom Riders, the Birmingham church bombing where four young black girls were killed, and much more.

When I retired and told my friends I was moving back to Alabama, they asked me why and voiced their concerns about the state because of its history. A month after I moved back and got settled, a couple of them came to visit to see where I lived and what Alabama is like. They admitted their surprise from what they saw and what they knew prior to coming to the state. I asked my friends if they thought I still lived in the backwoods and in the cotton fields because of the stories I had shared with them about the field and other experiences of the South. Their excitement from what they saw, expected, and experienced in

Alabama was hilarious. Maybe they thought I was going back in history and things were still the same. When they arrived and saw the same restaurants and department stores where they lived, they were in awe and admitted their naivete of Alabama. They saw what I saw and spoke of Alabama's beauty, the cost of living in comparison to where they were living, how friendly the people are, and the cleanliness of the state. They understood why I wanted to move back. One of them even contemplated moving here as well, but of course, I am still waiting for that.

School Days 59-60

I was a little black girl with long skinny legs, walking around, sucking her thumb, playing barefoot outside on the front yard that didn't have any grass, stepping on chicken poop, sometimes having it stick between the toes of her bare feet. No one could have ever made believe that my life would turn to a direction wherein I would someday walk beside or be in the company of some of the most powerful, prominent, and influential people of this country.

A native of Florence, Alabama, I lived in a community in Oakland—a neighborhood called the Black Jacks, today known as subdivisions or suburbs. This name, Black Jacks, was derived from the maple trees that grew in my neighborhood. Maple trees were plentiful in the area I lived and were covered with black spots. East of the Black Jacks was a road that divided my community called East End. Each community consists of blacks only. That may have been deliberate due to racial segregation.

Three-Room House

I grew up in a single-family home and lived in a three-room house with seven people. Yes, that's correct, three rooms with seven people: my mother, grandmother, and five children. I was the youngest of the five—four girls and one boy. My mom was the only one working to take care of seven people. My grandmother took care of us while Mama worked. Mama was called Mutt Dear, and our grandmother was called Big Mama. From time to time throughout my stories, you may hear Mutt Dear, Dear, Big Mama, Mama, or Mom, referring to the parents that raised me and my siblings.

Imagine seven people living in a three-room house. There were two bedrooms and a kitchen. There was no inside plumbing, and neither was there outside plumbing. Since then, I've lived in a house that had four bathrooms with only two people living in the house: my husband and myself. I don't think there was ever a time while living in that house with four-bathroom rooms that I didn't think about the times as a child that I didn't have a bathroom inside the house at all. No matter where I was in the house with four bathrooms, I could only use one. As crazy as it may sound, I could never use but one particular bathroom, and that was the one in my bedroom. This was a three-level house with twenty-six steps in it. There were thirteen steps from the bedrooms to the living room and kitchen and another thirteen steps from the kitchen and dining room to the family room in the basement. There were two bathrooms upstairs—one on the first level and one in the family room at the basement. If I was downstairs in the family room at the basement, I would climb twenty-six steps and bypass three bathrooms just to use the bathroom in my bedroom.

Those bathrooms were small in comparison to the size of the bathroom where we lived in our three-room house with seven people. The bathroom we used in the three-room house was the largest bathroom in the world—open and very spacious. Our bathroom was the open fields and woods in the country. To use the bathroom, you went into the woods and hid behind trees so that no one could see you in the surrounding area. We were not the only one using this open space, and yes, there were times when we would go to use the open space and see other neighbors there, but we would wait until we saw the person leave so we could go in to use the wood. Anyone having an outhouse was considered to have a luxury, but we were too poor to afford that.

In the modern times, you can say we had a powder room in our three-room house. As my siblings and I talk about these times, now we say we had two powder rooms. A powder room is a bathroom without a shower or tub. We had a foot tub, a deep bucket tub the size of a basin to wash up in during the morning, and a round tin tub deeper and wider for seated bathing and taking a bath at night. This same tub was used to do the laundry—our rendition of a bathtub and sink. A slop jar was the porta potty, today's modern commode. We all used the same slop jar, and in the morning, someone would take it out to dispose of the waste. Unfortunately, that someone was me. That became the household chore assigned to me by Mutt Dear. "To do other business" as we sometimes referred to it, you had to hold it in until the next day. Or if it was a night emergency and you couldn't hold it, Mutt Dear would make one of us go with the other outside into the field or woods as a bodyguard to keep away the night's creepy-crawlies and critters while we did our business. Remind you this was rural so there were no outside light and it was difficult to see much of anything.

Our three-room house was a warm, clean, and happy home, and I don't mean "warm" temperature-wise. There was so much love, joy, and happiness in that house with the seven of us. Big Mama was the matriarch of our family. She was the peacekeeper, comforter, and strength, the glue that held us together in spite of our living conditions. Big Mama had five children of her own. My mom was the youngest of Big Mama's five. Three of her children lived near us. And each Sunday, after church, her children would come to our three-room house, and they would bring their children and their children's children. We would get together, and there would be so much fun and laughter. The children would play softball in the field that was in front of our house, not the field that was sometimes used for our bathroom of course. The adults would sit on the porch, talking, watching us play, and encouraging each other team to win the game. Sometimes the adults would join us in playing softball, and that meant even more laughter. Seeing what we called the old folk at that time hit a ball and run to the base was hilarious and exciting because, to us, small children they were old. Looking back now, I realized they were young. Most of them were in their early twenties, and that was young. My mom was twenty-two years old when she had me, and I was the baby. Imagine having five children at twenty-two years old. That is a lot and a big responsibility, especially as a single parent.

As we gathered in the field, there would be so much noise and laughter that others families in the Black Jacks and East End—the other side of the community across the dirt road—would come and join us play ball. The more, the merrier because that brought more fun and laughter.

Our parents couldn't afford an actual ball and bat. Our bat was made from a tree branch that one of my uncles or some of the other community relatives had carved out of wood. The ball was made of rags that were stuffed together from old ones that some of the family member could no longer use or were worn beyond use. The rag ball was tied at the top in knots, so the stuffing of the rags on the inside would not fall out. All this fun and laughter took place in front of the three-room house that was clean and spotless.

When my uncles and aunts would come on Sundays with all their children, they didn't just come and sit on the front porch and talk while the children played softball. There would be a meal cooked by Big Mama. It wasn't an elaborate meal, but it was enough to feed all of us. When I look back on this, I asked myself how Big Mama was able to do this when no one in the house worked but Mutt Dear. Where did the food come from to feed that many people? Big Mama would cook what we called a gumbo. It was a large pot of mixed vegetables and one chicken that she had caught off the yard, killed, picked the feathers off, cleaned, and added to that pot of soup. The soup had plenty of water so it could feed all of us. Big Mama would cook a large skillet of corn bread to go with the soup, but she would make sure that we didn't take a large slice of the bread. She would tell us to get a small portion and crumble it up in the bowl of soup we were given, and that would fill us up. Big Mama taught us how to make food go a long way, and it wasn't about the amount but what you could do with the little you had.

Our three-room house was small, but to us, it appeared large. One of my uncles, Uncle Jack, built this house for us. It wasn't built with the best materials, but the foundation it was built upon was strong and lasting, and that foundation was the unity of family love. Our house was built out of planks, not the type of material that houses today are built of.

Planks are boarded piece of wood scraps that my uncle put together, created a design with by using his imagination, and constructed a suitable house from, which was presentable for living. What was so amazing and loving about our house was the love the house was built from. He built this house so that his mother, Big Mama, and his youngest sister, Mutt Dear, would have a place to live with her five children. He was married and had children of his own. This was the second house he built with his own hands, with the little he had to work with for the family he loved and cared so much. This was also the house that my siblings and I were born in.

Four of my siblings were born during the winter months. The twins were born in December, my brother and middle sister were born in January, and I was born in July.

I remember the winter months in the house. We would sit inside the house and look outside through cracks in the walls. Mutt Dear would bring newspapers and cardboard from work to cover the cracks in the walls and keep the heat in and cold out. We had a coal and wooden burner to keep us warm during the winter. I can remember sitting around the heater, laughing and cracking jokes with one another, and Big Mama sitting with us, sewing on a quilt in her lap and laughing with us while Mutt Dear was at work. If she was there, she would be in the next room, reading a book. One thing about Mutt Dear was that she loved to read and always had a book in her hand when she wasn't working. The books she read were given to her by people from her job or when someone left them in the room she cleaned. She definitely could not afford to buy them. Whenever she came home with a book left in a room, she would say someone left a treasure for her. What was one man's trash was another man's treasure. That was the first time I heard that phrase. She was thankful to get what was sometimes thrown in the trash or left lying on a bed at the hospital where she worked as a maid.

We were poor, but we didn't know that or may not have understood that concept. All I knew is that we were happy and there was so much love among us. If there was unhappiness, we didn't know it. Big Mama and Mutt Dear never discussed what they were going through or experiencing in front of us children. Now looking back, Mutt Dear wasn't always happy. With seven mouths to feed and having five stair steps, she didn't have time to think about anything but taking caring of us. Reading was her escape, and maybe that was why she read books all the time. We all were so close in age. In one year, she gave birth to three babies, and they weren't triplets.

The times were hard for my mom. One year she applied for public assistant before Christmas so that we could have something for Christmas. In the place she applied for, she was assigned a caseworker. When the process began, she was asked how many children she had and their dates of birth. When she told the person her children's dates of birth, the person who was assigned to take the information to determine if she qualified for the aid or not, disputed her and told her that she should be ashamed because she didn't know the dates of her children's births. Mutt Dear was told that there was no way that anyone could have three children born in the same year if they were not triplets. Mutt Dear tried to explain to her how this could and did happen, but the person was unable to comprehend how it happened. Mutt Dear said she was made to feel as if she was being called a liar and ignorant. She disputed what Mutt Dear said and told her she could not assist her until she gave the correct information needed of her children's births. Mutt Dear was told to go home and look at our birth certificates or bring them back if she had them so that she would know the correct dates of our birth and begin the application process over.

She said she left the place in tears, upset, but she never let the woman see her tears and how upset she was. There wasn't anything she could do but go home. Although she knew the dates we were born and the dates were correct, this woman insulted her and called her stupid in so many words. During that era, blacks didn't think they could talk back to white people. It was considered disrespectful. All they could do was bite their lip and do as told. This was in the early fifties during racial segregation, when whites thought they could talk and treat blacks in any type of way.

One thing about Mutt Dear was that she was far from being an ignorant woman. Reading books, she learned a lot and her vocabulary was broad. She left the place and went back the next day with copies of our birth certificates. The same caseworker was reassigned to her, and she was glad about that because she wanted to prove to her that she knew the dates her children were born. The woman assisting her told her that this was the first time she had ever heard of anyone having three children in one year. In place of apologizing to my mother, she further insulted her and told her she shouldn't have that many children if she couldn't take care of them, but the application was approved.

I don't think any of us children knew how underprivileged we were. If what you have is all you know, how can you miss what you never had? As a child, for as long as you're not hungry and you are happy, you think things are okay, especially when others around you have living conditions that are no different from yours.

Older people in those days had a lot of sayings. They would quote things that stuck with you throughout your life. Big Mama would say, "All the time you can be poor, but you didn't have to be nasty." Big Mama also taught a valuable lesson when sweeping the dirt yard. She taught us that no matter what you have and how you live, keep it clean and take care of it. Matthew 25:21 says that if you are faithful over a few things, God will make you ruler over many. Those three rooms in our small house stayed spotless. The front yard we played in that didn't have any grass and only had dirt stayed clean. If Big Mama saw a piece of paper or anything that didn't belong in that yard, which she thought would take away the cleanness or beauty from it, she would have us pick it up immediately.

Saturday was our day to clean the entire house and the yard. If there was any trash that the wind had blown in the yard or near the house, we had to pick it up. Afterward, the dusty dirt yard was to be swept with the broom. The furniture—what little of it we had—had to be dusted and polished with furniture oil. To this day, I can still smell the scent of the oil, just thinking of it. It was a clean, refreshing smell.

Sweeping the dirt yard and having dust blowing everywhere didn't make sense to me. I could not grasp that. Although I thought it was crazy and made no sense to me, I knew better than to verbally express my thoughts.

One of the sayings quoted often by Mutt Dear and Big Mama that would pop into my head is "There is a method to the madness." Whenever that comes into my mind, things I didn't understand became a fun game. I learned to challenge my mind to dissect things I didn't understand.

Big Mama was creative, and I realized this as I got older. She found ways to make whatever we did into something fun, and with that, we didn't mind doing whatever was asked of us. Summer storms were prevalent in the south. Sometime before a storm appeared, the wind would blow the dirt and the dust would form into circles of a whirlwind. A story Big Mama would tell us while sitting around the potbellied stove was that when a windstorm appeared, if you stuck a pin in the center of it, you could see the devil. Of course, curiosity got the best of us, and whenever a storm came, we would get a pin, go outside, and run through the dust with the pin, trying to see the devil. We never did see him, thank God, but that became a game for me and my siblings and not a job. After that story, we loved sweeping the dirt yard, just to stir up the dust, hoping to see the devil.

There was no money to buy toys and games. The environment taught us how to use resources and whatever was found freely lying around to our advantage and turn them into something fun. We utilized every resource we had to bring joy and laughter. We would find tires from old wagons, parts from old abandoned cars, and we would take pieces of wood and make go-carts to ride and play in. We would push the go-cart to the top of a hill. Someone would sit inside, and others would stand behind the go-cart and give it a shove, pushing it down the hill. The person inside would be yelling and laughing at the top of their lungs, and that would bring laughter from the rest of us. This was a neighborhood effort with children from both sides of the communities, the Black Jacks and East End. We came together as families and communities to build and create together. We all had joy and laughter sharing the little that we had.

We don't see much of this camaraderie anymore. Things have changed with time. People have more than they've ever had, but with that, so much has been lost. People have lost the camaraderie and love. Unity, friendship, families, communities, and even churches lost what was once so beautiful and precious. All these are almost a thing of the past, with love and laughter not too far behind from fading. Unity and laughter dissipated with the majority and not with one race or nationality. People as a whole have lost what is the most important. It makes you wonder what happened. It's sad to say, but when people had less, they seemed happier. The more people acquire, the less happy they seem. We give our children too much, and the more we give them, the less appreciative they seem to be. They don't know how to appreciate what they have and who gives them what they have.

Years back, people had little, but they knew how to appreciate and respect and love one another. Looking back and comparing what I call the "yonder years." Those were the good days. These yonder years were better than today. People have more today than they've ever had and yet no one seem to be happy anymore. Unfortunately, greed has tarnished the morals, values, and principles of families, society, and our government. A lack of having brought families and communities together when we look back. We can only ask, What happened? Where did the good times go? Good times meaning love, joy, laughter, and peace, not material things or the amount of money a person accumulates. The Bible tells us not to speak of the former days or good old days because both are the works of God's sovereign plan (Ecclesiastes 7:10, 13, 14).

Big Mama Passing

Mutt Dear, with the help of a friend, had a house built for us. We now lived in a four-room house. Uncle Jack, Mutt Dear's brother, and his wife, Aunt Callie, moved into the three-room house we had lived in, and he added more rooms to the house after they moved in. With Uncle Jack next door, the Black Jacks became perfect. More love and happiness were added to our lives. Mutt Dear and her brother were very close, and for Big Mama to have two of her children that close to her was joy.

A few years after moving into our new house, Big Mama had a stroke and passed away. After her passing, I began to notice the change that was taking place in our home. We felt her loss deeply. I admired my mother with five children. She always put us first. After Big Mama passed, Mutt Dear couldn't boil a pot of water, and boy, we suffered because she did not know how to cook. If it had not been for Aunt Callie, Mutt Dear's sister-in-law who lived next door, we would have starved. Aunt Callie taught her how to cook. When she came home from work, she would cook dinner and would let us eat first. Being children, we ate what we liked, and we left the rest on the plate. She never said a word until she thought we were finished eating, and then she would ask if we were finished. When we told her that we were finished, she would take what was left on our plates and eat. We didn't notice that right away, and it was a while before we did notice that she would eat the leftovers on the plates.

With Big Mama's passing, things started going in a different direction. The joy and laughter were taken away with her death. I was nine when she passed, and Mutt Dear became a little harder on us. The stress and responsibility of taking care of five children, working a full-time job, and not having any financial support took a toll on her emotionally and physically. The loss of her mother and the responsibility of five children with no one helping her were overwhelming. She began to assign to us the things Big Mama took care of like laundry, ironing, cooking, and cleaning. When she went to work, she left instructions that were to be followed and done by the time she got home from work. I never learned to cook, but I could clean the heck out of a house, and in doing that, I turned it into something fun. To this day, I still love cleaning.

Being the baby, I didn't think I had to do what the others did. I was very small and was super skinny. As my uncle Jack would always say whenever he saw me, I didn't even weigh ten pounds soaking wet. I didn't weigh fifty pounds for real, and my siblings didn't think I could do any of the work because of my size, so they did everything for me.

They spoiled me because Big Mama had spoiled me, and I milked that for every penny it was worth. If they said I couldn't do something, I put forth no effort to attempt to do it because I knew they would do it for me. Mutt Dear found out that my siblings were doing things for me, and she wasn't having it. She said they were making me lazy. Because we didn't have inside plumbing, the water we used to drink, cook, do laundry, and take baths was drawn from a well, or cistern, far from the house that was shared with others in the neighborhood. We had to go to the well and carry water in buckets back and forth for use. My siblings thought the bucket filled with water was too heavy for me to carry, so they carried it for me. Mutt Dear noticed them carrying my bucket and put a stop to that quick. She made me carry my own bucket.

Picking Cotton

During the summer before school started, we went to the fields to pick cotton to help buy our school clothes. Cotton harvesting in the South usually began during the month of September. In the midfifties, cotton was picked by field hands (human beings). Owners of the cotton were familiar with the community and knew who would pick for them because those who worked at the cotton gin where the cotton was processed and stored were families from the Black Jacks and East End community, which were predominantly black. Therefore, when it was harvesttime, it was families of those that worked for the owners who picked the cotton. Owners of the fields would come early in the morning, driving a pickup truck and stopping by each house to pick up those who were to pick the cotton. We would sit in the back of the truck, and sometimes there would be so many of us that some had to sit in the cab of the truck with the owner. We would be packed in the back of the truck like sardines or herds of cattle going to the slaughter.

We were picked up between 6:45 to 7:00 a.m., and we stayed in the fields until sunset, which was around 5:30 p.m. to 6:00 p.m. From sunup to sundown, the heat in the middle of the day would be unbearable, but we didn't pay attention to the heat because our focus was to pick as much cotton as we could to bring home as much money as we could to buy school clothes. The amount of money made depended upon the amount of cotton picked per pound. I went to the field to have fun and to play. There again I used my size as an excuse not to work. I guess you can say it was because of Big Mama. Although she was no longer with me, she turned everything we did into fun and game, so I still had that mind-set after her death. My siblings had me thinking I didn't have to pick as much cotton as they did because of my size, so I played all day in the field until Mutt Dear put her foot down about that as well and gave me a quota—a set amount that she expected me to pick daily. One particular day, I was in the field, and I picked less than twelve pounds the entire day. At quitting time that evening, when everyone would go to the wagon where the owner would add up what each person picked for that day to pay them for their work, when they got to me and called my name to be paid, I was told I had picked only twelve pounds. One of the workers, his name was Mr. Early, knew my mom told me, "You know what you're going to get when you get home." I knew I was going to get a whipping. I began crying right there and cried all the way home. I didn't make ten cents that day, so the owner felt sorry for me and gave me a quarter.

The twins could pick two hundred pounds of cotton a day. My middle sister, Amie, and my brother William could never pick as much as the twins. My quota was fifty pounds a day, and that day, I picked only twelve pounds. I knew I was going to get my butt whipped. When we got home from the field, we would give our money to Mutt Dear to put away for our school clothes. I was so scared to give her my 0.25 cents, and when I did, she asked if this was all I had. I began crying ever harder. I told her I had been sick all day and had lain on my cotton sack and on the twins'—Osie and Ree—sack because I wasn't feeling good. But she wasn't buying any of that. She made me go outside and get a switch off a tree. It was punishment enough to get a whipping. Having to go get your own switch for someone to beat your butt was more painful than getting the whipping.

Parents didn't have a problem whipping children during that era, and it worked for the better for those who were raised during that time. Today is a different story. Spare the rod, and spoil the child (Proverbs 13:24). Whipping or spanking a child even your own today can put you in jail or have them taken from you. Spanking or whipping children during this era was the way parents raised their children. To say that it was right or wrong is a matter of opinion. One thing is for sure: there is a notable gap in the children of today's generation and the children of that era. Discipline is necessary and should be used. Discipline today is comical to children, and this is why you don't get respect from many of them and why they don't take anything seriously. Some things should not be changed, and if the type of discipline of yesteryear were reinstated, we would see a difference in today's children and those to come.

Getting my own switch and getting the whipping that I still remember to this day changed my thought process and made me know what it means to work. The next day, I went to the field and picked over fifty pounds of cotton. I could have picked 50 lbs each day but I wanted to play because that's what I was made to think I didn't have to work. I had gotten it into my head that I didn't have to do as my siblings did because I was the baby.

This experience taught me three things. If I had continued to use my size as an excuse that I couldn't do certain things, that thought process could have handicapped me for the rest of my life. Second, the experience taught me to set goals for myself. And third, it taught me that I can do anything once I set my mind to it. I didn't understand at the time what my mother was doing, but she was teaching me goals and work ethic. My mother had many philosophies in life, and one of her philosophies was if you are going to do anything, do it right or don't do it at all. When she told me I had to pick fifty pounds of cotton, she was showing me how to set goals. In order to achieve something or anything you want, you have to have a vision. Setting goals makes you look inside yourself, see your capabilities, and learn to maximize your potentials. Hindsight is a powerful thing once you recognize and see what is before you. You don't understand things when they first happen, but hindsight is the key that unlocks insight and takes you higher to further accomplishments. People get trapped into settling for the minimum because they are not forced or put into a position to achieve. You have to learn who you are in order to move forward in life, and you learn by doing.

When I came home from the field the next day and gave my mom more than a quarter, it made me proud and I felt good about myself. I was proud because I had achieved something that I did not know I was capable of, and the next day, I was even more excited because I knew I would do more and better than the day before. I told myself that I could and I would, and guess what, I did exactly that. I did better than the day before. If I had never been put into that position, I would never have known what I was capable of. It made me want more, do more, and go to the next level. I was eleven years old at the time, and being in the cotton field all day made me realize I was capable of doing much more in life. I knew I had something in me that wants more and does more, but I didn't know how to make it come alive.

Everything in life, in order to make it fit so that you could succeed, takes strategic thinking and planning. Going to the cotton fields with set goals and planning how much cotton I would pick made me think about what I could do when school started again. I was excited about school starting, and I looked forward to applying that principle when learning my school lessons. The cotton field was the beginning of my adult learning. I realized that everything you do takes strategic planning.

The theory "There's a method to madness" taught me what to do when I arrived at the cotton field to begin my day. You wanted to be next to a person whom you knew was good at picking cotton and whom you could talk with and not be left behind. Some could pick cotton faster than others, and they would pick so fast they would get ahead of you and left you with no one to talk to, so you had time to think. My problem was that I would think and daydream a little too much and too long. Sometimes I would get so far behind the person I started out with that morning that when they looked back to see where I was, they would begin picking cotton from my row so that I could catch up with them. Or they would yell and tell me to come on and catch up.

I was a slow picker, and I had plenty of time to think. I remember thinking to myself that there had to be something better to life than picking cotton. I don't know where this dream or vision came from, but I remember saying that I was going to travel the world and that I was going to be a model. I dreamed about going to London and Paris. I had no idea what London or Paris looked like. I may have had only known them from the images of what I heard in school or from the stories my mom would share from the books she read. These visions and fantasies played around in my head while I was in the field. The heat from the sun beaming down on my head could have caused those visions or thoughts, but they were happy and pleasant thoughts that excited me.

A vision can remain a vision if it's just a thought, but once something is spoken into the atmosphere, it can become a reality and be put into action. Proverbs 18:21 says, "Life and death is in the power of the tongue." Proverbs 23:7 says, "So that a man thinketh so is he." Being in those cotton fields made me become a thinker. I became a dreamer because it helped pass the time, and before I knew it, I completed the rows of cotton I was picking and my sack was filled to the point that I couldn't put any more into it. It was time to take it to the weight station to be weighed, and I could start that process all over again and begin dreaming more dreams. My dream was to get out the cotton fields. I knew that was something I could not and would not see myself doing until I finished school. There had to be something better. I learned to plan and think ahead of the cotton fields, and everything I've done in life since I still plan and think ahead.

Mutt Dear and Big Mama did not have much, and they had very little education. What they had they taught us, they taught with mother wit. Mother wit is nothing more than good old common sense.

A high school diploma doesn't compare with what and how they taught us. They taught morals, standards, principles, and values. Things I learned from them taught me how to survive in a world when I didn't have a college degree. So many have gone to college and gotten a degree or more but are just as ignorant as the day they were born. You can't tell them a thing because it's all about their degree. Those who put their degree before anything else in life is stuck in being a fool with a degree. Don't get me wrong; there is nothing wrong with a college degree, but college degrees have ruined some people. They think their degree is the power to life. Some have gone to college and graduated and still can't read as well as a first grader. They paid their way through school by allowing someone to take exams for them. Or if their parents were wealthy, they made it on the monetary donation their parents paid to the institution. The most valuable thing I learned about college is that a college graduate without G-O-D is a phenomenal fool. There are many unintelligent people—some running our country and have a degree but have no common sense. The whipping I got from picking twelve pounds of cotton taught me how to challenge myself in any position I was put in. It taught me I could do anything I set my mind to. I learned that if there was something I wanted, I had to know what it takes and what I have to do to get it—and that is to work hard and use common sense. Common sense will take you further than any degree.

I had a job where I was accountable for maintaining a 2.3-million-dollar budget even if I didn't have a college degree, which I will go into more detail further into the book. Math was my worst subject in school, but with common sense, I mastered that budget and did it well.

SHIRLEY NOEL ADKINS

Racist Experiences as a Teenager

County School Counselor

The stigma associated to Alabama makes people think the worst. People think negatively of Alabama because of its history. Many horrendous, cruel, and racial injustices happened before and after segregation, which left burning memories in the minds of people. The name Alabama, whenever mentioned, rekindle painful and negative memories and images for so many people, especially to those who lived up in the North: Governor George Wallace, the march to Selma, the bombing of the Church in Birmingham, which killed five little black girls, to name a few. Racism still remains but in a subtle type of way.

I attended West End High, an all-black school, up until my junior year 1968. Attending an all-black school had benefits and downfalls. The benefit of attending an all-black school was that everyone was equal. The only racism we experienced was through the school system. The downfalls were not the faculty's fault because of racism and segregation. What was privy to the white school was not privy to the black schools. Black schools were not given proper educational tools for students to learn. The books we were given were secondhand books from the previous years' white students in white schools. By the time books were sent to the black schools, they were in such poor condition and not fit for use. The front or back covers of the books were torn, and pages were missing and marked through. It's hard to teach when you don't have the necessary tools and equipment, but our teachers did the best they could with what they had.

The majority of blacks who attended West End were underprivileged, and those who were considered middle-class could be counted on the fingers in one hand. I don't think we even knew what middle class was at the time. To me, we were all the same.

There were some children who did have both parents at home, and that was supposed to be considered middle-class because two incomes were coming into the home, but the majority of the students were from single-family homes. I can't remember hearing anyone talk about going to college, not to say that some didn't. I didn't talk to my mom about college, nor can I remember any of my siblings mentioning college. Maybe they thought—like I did—that she would have to pay out of her pocket to send me to college, and I knew she could not afford it. No one ever talked about college because we didn't know that there were programs that would help send us to college. Later, after I graduated, I found out about programs that could help send you to college. I wonder why we were never told these things. Did the faculty at the black school know about the programs? I assumed they didn't know, or maybe they did and also thought that our parents couldn't afford to send us to college because even with the programs, you still needed money.

Once there was a counselor that came to our school—a white female. We were told by the school principal that the county was sending someone from the board of education to come and talk with some of the students. She didn't talk with everyone, and she met those whom she talked with in the school library—something you never forget as a child. This was one of those things I can recall vividly.

The principal, B. W. Buckingham, whose name still resonates with everyone who ever attended West End, said to us that this counselor wanted to talk with some students and that she would be asking us questions. There would be a selective few chosen that she would talk with. He wanted us to be polite, to speak intelligently, and to answer the questions she would ask us. I don't know how the process took place or how the selective few were chosen. We had no idea what she would be asking, and I don't recall if the principal knew what she would be asking. If he did, he never gave us any indication or advance notice. I remember some of us being afraid and hoping we would not be chosen to meet with this person. As luck would have it, I was one of the chosen. I was selected to speak with her.

She met with me, and she started asking me about my family, if there were two parents in my home, how many children were in my family, how I was treated at home, if I liked school, and what I wanted to do when I finished school. I remember being very scared, and I wondered why she was asking such personal questions. How I was being treated at home and if my siblings were being treated the same. When she asked me what I wanted to do when I finished school, that's when I became excited because this was my opportunity to do as Mr. Buckingham had said, which was to speak intelligently. When she asked what I wanted to do, I answered with excitement and said to her I wanted to be a gynecologist. The look she gave me made me feel as if I had said and done something horribly wrong. I remember feeling embarrassed and scared at the same time because I thought I had said something wrong. I could get in trouble for saying what I had spoken. Mr. Buckingham told us to talk and speak intelligently and give intelligent answers, so I thought she would be impressed with what I told her.

Knowing now what "being outside the box" means, I can say I have always thought outside the box. Being in the cotton field taught me how to do that. She looked me in my eyes and told me I could forget that because that was something that would never happen since I had to go to college to do that. Negroes didn't go to college because they couldn't afford it and I wasn't smart enough.

She asked me where I got that word from and if I knew what a gynecologist was. I told her my mother worked at a hospital and that sometimes when she came home, she would tell us the most exciting stories about some of the doctors and what they did. Then she wanted to know what type of work my mother did, and when I told her she was a maid, she proceeded to tell me being a maid is what I could do better than being a gynecologist. She told me to forget that and never say it again. She said that after I finished school, more than likely I would work as a maid because whatever one's parents did, that was what their children would end up doing and that was as close as I would ever get to a gynecologist—by working in a hospital as a maid. Mutt Dear worked as a housekeeper (maid) at a hospital. She talked about how unclean people were and how she had to clean up behind them. I knew that was something I didn't want to do. I did not understand or know what this was at the time, but I am OCD. I couldn't stand filth or other people's nastiness, so I knew I could never do that type of work. I never liked being around certain things that I considered nasty. I've always been organized and couldn't stand seeing things out of place, especially in the house I live or in the office I work. It was only in recent years that I learned the term OCD and learned its meaning.

Mutt Dear worked at the hospital in housekeeping and some nights as we were sitting around the stove keeping warm, she would share stories about what she had seen at the hospital. She talked about some of the doctors and the things she would hear them talking about. I remember her talking about OB-GYN and the gynecologist and the babies in the nursery after they were born, which all fascinated me. I fantasized about being that type of doctor and what it was like to deliver babies. Although I knew I could never be one, it fascinated me and it sounded good. I thought telling the counselor that I wanted to be a doctor would impress her and make her think I was smart. To say that it crushed my spirit is to say the least. From that time on, I never played with that fantasy or spoke those words again.

After I was told this, it was like my mind erased itself. I felt like the writings on a chalkboard after you take an eraser and wipe them out. I was a child, and this came from a white person, so I thought I had done and said something wrong. I thought she would tell Mr. Buckingham what I had said and that I would get in trouble with him and Mutt Dear.

Looking back over this makes me wonder a lot of things now. Over the years, I wondered if what she said to me was intentional and deliberate. In her mind, did she genuinely and truly believed what she told me was right? Did she believe that blacks didn't attend college to become doctors, or was that her way to tell me to stay in my place because she thought blacks had a certain place in society and being a doctor wasn't one of them?

Maybe she didn't know what a gynecologist was, and that was why she asked me where I heard the word and if I knew what it means. Was this deliberate to brainwash me into thinking that being a maid was the only thing I had to look forward to? Was this the strategy used to brainwash blacks to put them in a mental place, keep them down and inferior, and keep a slavery mentality so that we could never become anything but someone washing, cleaning, and cooking for whites? If you think beyond or above the norm, that makes them think you feel superior and equal to them.

I learned a valuable lesson from that. I learned to never speak something just to impress someone, and I learned to never share a dream or vision with just anyone. People can kill your dreams if you allow them to. Who knows what could have happened if she had encouraged me instead of discouraging me? How many other dreams from students she met with that day did she destroy?

I never shared what happened that day with anyone because I was afraid I had said something wrong and could have gotten in trouble. My seventh grade homeroom teacher, Mrs. Fannie M. Smith, whom I love and owe so much to even to this day, spoke something into me that stayed with me through life. What she spoke was right after what was spoken to me by this counselor. God knows what we need and when we need it. What Mrs. Smith spoke to me was medicine of healing for wounded soul. I can't remember how long it took—from what the counselor said to what Mrs. Smith said. When your spirit is broken and something hurt you, it shows up in some form: through your character, physically, emotionally, or mentally. Or it may have shown up in my classwork.

What was said to me by this counselor took something out of me, and maybe Mrs. Smith noticed that something was amiss with me. With her being my homeroom teacher, she knew my demeanor and she knew that something wasn't the same. For days after the meeting with the counselor, I waited to be called into the office by Mr. Buckingham to be chastised because of what I said to her. Mrs. Smith called me to her desk one morning before it was time to exchange classes. Her calling me up to her desk scared me. I thought she was going to ask me about what took place with the counselor, but she didn't mention it.

She said to me, "Shirley, you have great potential, and you're going to succeed and achieve great things in life."

I could not wait for the bell to ring so that I could go to the library and look up the meaning of *potential* and excel because I wasn't sure if I knew the meaning of what she had spoken to me but I knew it sound good.

After going to the library and looking up the words and understanding the meaning, no one could ever tell me anything about what I could or could not do ever again. From that point on, I thought I could do anything. I began putting more effort into my studies to make better grades because I did not want to disappoint Mrs. Smith. She believed in me and saw potential. Being my homeroom teacher, she would see all my grades before I got them. Other teachers whom I had classes with sent her the grades that I would make in their classes. She would compile all my grades onto my report card. I never knew if what was said by this counselor was said to other students or if the principal and faculty found out. I was happy, and Mrs. Smith restored what was nearly destroyed in me that day.

Corner Store

Seeing the way Big Mama was treated taught and gave me my first awareness into racism. One thing about adult of the yonder years is that there were certain things that were not talked about in front of or around children. When grown people were having conversations, children were made to leave the room. For a child to get into grown-people conversation was definitely a no-no. Sure, adults had conversation about things that they thought a child should not listen to, and being children, we pretended to leave the room and not listen, but you can be assured that little ears were wide open and tuned in even though you were asked to leave the room. As a child, I overheard something Big Mama and other grown-ups would talk about concerning racism. I was very young, but I was old enough to realize and understand that she was being disrespected just because of the color of her skin. That was one of the things I learned and overheard when asked to leave the room. She was having a conversation and was sharing the incident with Mrs. Mae Ola, one of her neighbors that lived across the field what happened to her at the corner store.

There was a small neighborhood corner grocery store near us. Most times, Big Mama would take me or one of my other siblings with her as she walked to the store. The people who owned the corner store were white and young enough to be Big Mama's grandchildren. When they talked to her, she would say, "Yes, sir," "No, sir," "Yes, ma'am," and "No, ma'am" to them. She addressed them in that manner because that was required during that era—blacks addressing whites with respect, so to speak. They addressed her as Amie, which was her first name, and to me, that was disrespectful because of her age. I watched her face as she was being talked to, and I saw a look that I could not identify at the time. But I knew it was something she didn't like and that it hurt her. Seeing that hurt on her face upset me, and I kept asking her what was wrong.

"Yes, ma'am," "No, ma'am," "No, sir," and "Yes, sir" are a courtesy saying for Southerners to those who are older than you. Race had nothing to do with it, or so I thought. We were taught to say that from Mutt Dear and Big Mama. I always said, "No, ma'am" and "Yes, ma'am" to Big Mama, so why weren't the people at the store saying it to her? Why was she addressing them the way they should have been addressing her? I was taught to respect elders regardless of the color of their skin, and I thought it was automatic for everyone if they were your elder.

The boy at the store couldn't have been more than a year or so older than me, and I was around six or seven years old at the time. I knew Big Mama addressing him "Yes, sir" and "No, sir" was wrong. As I replayed these incidents in my mind, I remember he had a cloth in his hand, which he used to dust the canned goods on the shelves at the store. Rat droppings and dust were always on the canned goods. The cans were old, rusty, and full of dust all the time. Thinking back now, I am sure the expiration dates on those canned goods were as old as me, but back then, I doubt if anyone ever thought about or knew of an expiration date. You could tell they had been there for a while.

He took the dust cloth; or the dust rag as we called it, that he was using to dust and wipe off the cans when he was talking to Big Mama and tossed the rag in my face. He said to her, "Look, Amie, at all this s—— and dust. She should be back here dusting these cans."

I wanted to fight him and slap rat droppings on his butt, but Big Mama laughed with him and shrugged it off.

When we left the store, I guess she could see how angry and upset I was, so she told me before I could ask her why he did what he did. She said to me. I had to take what he said so she could continue getting food for us. She had a store credit there, and if she had reacted any differently to what he did, they would have cut off her store credit. This boy's parents owned the store, and they allowed Big Mama to get things there on credit if she didn't have the money right then to pay for what she needed. She suffered humiliation, disrespect, and embarrassment form a child to keep food on our table. Mutt Dear would pay the bill at the end of the week or month when she got paid.

Big Mama was my heartbeat. There is something about grandparents that is indescribable. Children love their mom and dad, but there is something about grandparents especially grandmothers that are so special you can't put words to. It's unexplainable. Big Mama was so special she had a way with her that made you feel like you were the only person in the world. I thought I was her only and favorite grandchild, but as I got older, I found out that she made all her grandchildren feel the same way.

Her nurturing, protective, and sheltering spirit made you feel safe and secure, as if nothing could harm you. She was Big Mama, a grandmother who wore an apron and brown cotton stockings rolled up to her knees. I remember so vividly when I was outside playing. And if I fell and hurt myself, I would go to her crying. She would open up her arms and carry me. When I walked into her arms, she would wrap me in her apron. The way she wrapped her apron around me was medicine to my bumps, bruises, and boo-boos. It was comfort and protection, and it made all the difference in the world. Her apron was my escape and safety net when I was about to get my butt in trouble with Mutt Dear. If I did something that caused me to get my butt spanked, I would run to Big Mama. She would wrap me in her apron, and I would know I was safe, having escaped punishment from the switch. I was nine when she passed, and after her death, I lost my protection from the wrath of Mutt Dear's spanking and the world's abuse.

Rosa Park Experience

In the early sixties, it was very rare for rural areas to have a community transportation bus service. This was private-owned and operated by a family out of Waterloo in the west of Florence. The bus would take passengers from the rural communities into the city limits. Most people in the rural communities did not have automobiles and depended on this bus service to get them to and from their destination into the city limits for various reasons. There were few designated bus stops and pickup points. Wherever you stood on the side of the road and wherever the driver saw you, he would stop to pick you up. The bus fare was five cents per person each trip.

One particular day, I was standing at the road, waiting for the bus to go into the city. I was to meet Mutt Dear because I had to go to the doctor. I had fallen when I was in school and had a deep gash into my leg. I had to go back to the doctor for a follow-up consultation on getting the stitches removed. The bus driver saw me and stopped to pick me up. Keep in mind that this was during segregation, and blacks were to sit at the back of the bus, regardless if it was empty or full. This particular day, there were no passengers on the bus. I was the only one. As I got on and paid my fare, the driver took off before I could reach the back to take my seat. I lost my balance and fell into the seat directly behind the driver.

I remember thinking to myself, *Since I am here, I might as well sit until he stops again for the next passenger, and then I will move to the back just in case I lose my balance again.*

As that crossed my mind, I saw the driver look up at me in the rearview mirror. He didn't say anything at first. Maybe he was giving me time to get my balance and move, but I sat there. Since he didn't say anything, I thought maybe he could see the logic why I wasn't moving and knew I would move once he stopped for the next passenger, but that didn't happen.

He slammed his brakes and looked at me again in the rearview mirror and said to me, "Gal, you belong in the back."

I didn't say a word. I knew what he meant, so I got up to move to the rear. I knew I wasn't supposed to be there. I honestly can't say to this day that I knew I didn't belong there, but I also believe I sat there to see if I could sit there and to see what it felt like. It didn't feel any different from sitting in the back.

I saw this movie once. I can't remember the name of the movie, but it was about a little black boy who wanted to drink out of a white water fountain because he wanted to see if the water tasted different. When he finally got the nerves to drink from the fountain, he realized, too, that the water tasted the same as the water that came from the fountain that said, "For colored only." As I was watching this movie, it brought back memories of me sitting at the front of the bus.

I could not comprehend why blacks had to sit at the back of the bus when the bus was empty. I knew by the time we made it to our destination in the city, hardly anyone was on the bus—maybe one or two passengers because this was midday and most of the people who rode the bus were already at work. The bus would be crowded in the evening on the way back because everyone got off at the same time and taking the bus was the only means of transportation they had to get home if they didn't own their own vehicle, which mostly the case.

The majority of the people riding the bus were black. The front of the bus was never full. There was a cutoff point where blacks were allowed to sit, and if the black section was full and there were empty seats in the front, blacks still could not sit in that section and would have to stand even though there were empty seats available for someone to sit on. I guess that was another way of making blacks feel inferior and of reminding them of their place and that they should never cross the boundaries that were set by the white man.

Senior Year Expulsion:

1968 my junior year of high school, I had to attend Central High, an all-white school. West End, the all-black school I attended, was closing due to integration. That was an emotionally interesting and somewhat frightening transition. There was always the fear of the unknown. Going to an all-white school, I had many things running through my mind, and rightfully so. Seven years prior to that, George Wallace, the governor of Alabama, stood in the door at the University of Alabama to block the black students from entering. If the governor of the state felt that way, I knew that feeling just didn't stop there with him; it was felt throughout the state. I had experiences with racial discrimination that I thought was unspeakable, but to experience it in a classroom from a teacher was beyond comprehension.

At Central High, my American History teacher, Mr. Branscome, caused me to be expelled for two days during my senior year. That was the first time I was ever expelled from school, and I thought it would precede me for life and ruin my creditability for employment once I finished school. If this situation would have taken place today, this teacher would have lost his job, but then again maybe not. As I was going to my history class this particular day, I saw Patricia, a girl I had gone to school with all my life, beginning at West End. She came to me as we were changing classes, crying and telling me that Mr.

Branscome said some horrible things about blacks and that the other students began looking at her and laughing about it. She was the only black student in his class during that period. She told me to be prepared because she was sure he was going to say the same things again because he taught the same lesson each period. There was one other black student in my history class, Charles, who had attended West End with me as well. We were the only two people of color in this class.

As the class began and after the roll was called, Mr. Branscome began teaching. He began talking about slavery. I didn't know what that was all about or how black history was even brought up in class because black history was seldom taught in the South, if at all. He began by saying, "When Nigg-russ…" That word set me on edge and put me in a defensive mode instantly because of what had happened with Patricia. Once he said that, I knew then what was about to take place, he said "Nigg-russ," not Negroes.

He proceeded to say, "When they did something wrong, they were taken into the woods and hanged from a tree."

Some of the students began laughing and snickering and looking directly at me and Charles, like Patricia said they had done to her. At that point, I lost control. I thought about Patricia crying, and I was hurt and angry that they were laughing at me and Charles. I jumped up from my desk so fast that I nearly turned the desk over, and I called him a liar and told him the word wasn't "Nigg-russ" and if he was going to use the word, he should learn to pronounce it correctly. The word is *Negro* and not "nigg-russ." That was his subtle way of him calling us niggers and making what took place humorous. There wasn't anything funny about hanging someone. When I spoke out and said this to him, he ordered me out of his class and told me to go to the office and stay there until his class was over and he would join me afterward. I went to the office and told the principal, Mr. Brewer, what had taken place before he got there. The principal didn't say anything. He just told me to have a seat and wait until the teacher got there.

When he arrived, he told his side of what happened, and of course, he disputed what I said. He said he was teaching the lesson as it was written in history and didn't use the term as I described. Mr. Brewer told me I was disrespectful and that I had to be reprimanded and given a two-day suspension from school. I wanted to know what was going to be done about Mr. Brascome, and he said he would handle that, but nothing ever happened because he continued to teach and was teaching the next day while I was suspended.

After I went back to school from being suspended, I returned to his class. Nothing else was ever said or taught about black history again. I made all As in this class and was exempted from taking final exams at the end of the school year.

Mutt Dear Response To School Expulsion

After I came home and told Mutt Dear I was suspended from school for two days, she didn't give me the chance to explain in detail what happened and why I was suspended. She beat my butt without giving me the opportunity to explain what happened. She always knew I had plenty of mouth and didn't take too much of anything. I would express myself and let you know how I felt. I was very vocal at Central High when I thought there was unfair treatment against students of color. I was outspoken and tried to stage a protest at a pep rally because while blacks were allowed to play sports, especially football, none of the girls could participate as cheerleaders or be in the pep squad.

I would go home from school and tell my mom about this, and she told me to keep my mouth shut because that was my last year of school and that if I kept raising questions, I could cause problems that would get me suspended and that this would be on my school records, which would precede me wherever I went. She told me it didn't matter how we were treated as long as I completed my education. She also wanted to know if any of the other black students were saying anything, but of course she knew I was the most vocal. She called me the ringleader.

Black parents believed in beating their children. I said beating because that was how they punished us. I believed this punishment was duplicated from how our ancestors were punished during slavery. They just didn't realize that it was a replica of slavery and punishment transferred over into their own race. When I was expelled, I got my butt beat. I was beaten with a tree branch that was taken from a tree, which we called switches back then. Those branches left scars on you for days. It would break your skin open and cause you to bleed. I got a beating that day, and I was so glad I was out of school for two days because I had scars on me that could be seen. By the third day, when I went back to school, the scars were not as visible, but I wore long sleeves to cover the scars on my arms. My mother had to go to the school to meet with the principal before I could get back in. When she went to the principal's office, I was allowed to return to class. I didn't see my mom after she left the principal's office. It was there that she found out what actually happened during my expulsion.

I didn't see her until I got home from school that evening, and then she told me about her visit with the principal. She told me she was looking for a call from the school because after she found out what was said and why I was suspended, she got upset with the principal and wanted to see my history teacher. But she wasn't allowed to. She asked me why I didn't tell her what happened. I told her I tried to tell her, but she wasn't listening because she thought I was suspended because of racial protest I had told her previously about the pep rallies. She was livid. But she then apologized to me for not listening to me.

That was the first time my mom ever apologized to me for anything. I knew that hurt her. I overheard her telling Aunt Callie about it afterward, and that was one of those times I had my ears to the door even if children weren't supposed to be within listening range when adults were talking.

The thing that made me feel good was when I heard her tell Aunt Callie, and she called my teacher an ugly name. She said, "The bastard made me whip my baby for nothing." She wanted to go to the school and beat his ass. I got the biggest kick out of that, and that made me feel better. Mutt Dear had a potty mouth. I guess that's where I got mine from. I thought a potty mouth was the norm, depending on whom you were talking with. I did know when to and when not too use my potty mouth. Around her and other adults, I knew not to.

State Fair

Every year before school started, there would be a state fair with games and rides and hundreds of people. It was always crowded, and sometimes, people would bump into one another. My middle sister, Amie, and I were together walking around, seeing what rides we would ride next. All of a sudden, a white man and I bumped into each other. He reeked of alcohol and was drunker than Cootie Brown's cousin, as the saying goes in the South. He said to me, "Watch where you're going, Nigga," and he slapped the fire out of me before I could open my mouth. He slapped me so hard I saw flashes of light cross my eyes. I had heard the phrase "I was hit so hard I saw stars" many times; well, I experienced the reality of seeing stars for real after he hit my face that hard. It happened so quickly I was taken aback. It took me a second to realize what had taken place. As I realized what had happened and who it was that had hit me, my brain automatically went into a retaliation-and-com-bat response. As I looked around for something to pick up and knock the fire out of him, a man out of nowhere appeared and took the man who had slapped me away. I discovered that this man was a police officer in plain clothes. The officer, a white male of course, didn't ask me if I was okay or anything, and that made me angrier. I began crying, and I was upset with my sister because she didn't come to my defense. She told me, "Let's go," but I wanted to fight that man.

My brother was at the fair, and I began looking for him. I was still crying when I found him. I told him what happened, and he and I began looking for the man but couldn't find him. I don't know if he was escorted off the property by the police. As I looked back on this during family gatherings, when my siblings and I would get together and talk about childhood experiences and this particular incident came up, I am now glad we didn't find this man because I knew that if we had, someone would have gotten seriously hurt or killed.

My brother didn't play, and he always carried a knife on him even at a young age. He and I were the aggressors among our siblings, so I know what would have taken place, and it wouldn't have been good.

Being Shot At

My potty mouth and aggressiveness could have gotten me killed. Racial experiences can take you to a place of anger and bitterness, and if you're not careful, it can put something in your heart that hurts so bad that you may not be able to walk away from it. I had one of those experiences at a car dealership in the seventies. I had purchased my first car, a used one, and it kept giving me problems. I carried it back twice, and the third time I took it back, the service department wanted to charge me a towing fee. They didn't charge me for repairs because I got the car less than a month ago. After a third visit, when I went to pick it up, I was charged. I told the sales representative it was under a warranty because I got the car less than thirty days ago, but they told me they towed it in this particular time so I had to pay the towing fee or I couldn't get my car. I asked for a manager, and the man that came up to me was an older white man. From the way he approached me, I knew it was going to be difficult from the start. Sometimes you can tell from the way a person carries themselves what type of interaction you will have with them. It was something in his entire demeanor and facial expression that I knew he would be difficult to deal with.

He was sarcastic, arrogant, and indignant from the beginning and was adamant that I would not get my car unless I paid for it being towed. I tried explaining to him that the car was driven to the shop and that someone followed me there and that was why I was able to leave the car for a few days. The situation escalated and turned very ugly. He thought he could talk to me any kind of way and that I would accept his demand. When you've been verbally and mentally abused, you never forget it. At this point, being an adult living on my own and taking care of myself, the way I was approached and the tone in which he talked to me brought back some memories that I wasn't aware were sitting dormant inside and were not healed. He kept calling me a liar and said I owed the money. The only way I was going to get the car was I had to pay the towing fee. It was raining, and I had an umbrella with a glass handle in my hand. I told the manager if he called me a liar one more time, I would knock the hell out of him. He called me a liar again, and before I knew it, I hit him with the glass handle of the umbrella in my hand. Blood spewed from his forehead. He ran back inside the office. I assumed he left because blood was running down his face. By then, another person came out of the office, handed me my keys, and told me to leave. I took the keys and turned to walk away. The next thing I knew, I heard a gunshot. As I looked back, I saw the man I had hit pointing a gun at me. I turned and started walking back toward him with the gun still in his hand and told him if he wanted to shoot me, I would stand there.

He turned and ran back inside the building, and they locked the shop doors. I stood outside, knocking on the glass door and yelling at the man who was still standing there with the gun and bleeding from his forehead. I told him to open the door and shoot me. It was a glass door. I could see them, and they could see me. I was enraged, and at that moment, I didn't care if I lived or died. I had reached that place of anger, frustration, and bitterness of being treated any kind of way because of the color of my skin. That is the place I spoke of, where your heart and mind can take you when hurt and anger build up. After a while, it will spill over and out. After I left the car dealership, I thought about what had taken place. I called myself a fool and realized that I could have been killed. I was by myself. The person who took me to the dealership dropped me off and left me. No one would have known what happened to me. I was so angry at that moment. I didn't think about what could have happened to me. Anger took over my sense of reasoning, and I just knew that not another white person was going to talk to me with disrespect. No one called the police, and I don't know what happened to the man I hit in the forehead. I assumed that I was in the right and never heard anything else about the incident from anyone.

Racism never stops. You learn how to challenge your experiences and emotions, and God knows I've had my share. All life experiences prepare and equip us for our journey. My cotton-field experience was just the beginning of growth and maturity to face life's challenges and my destiny from the cotton fields to Capitol Hill. We learn by doing. The amazing thing about life is that we think we know what we want and how we are going to go about getting what we think we want. But your life is not your own because we were created and designed with purpose. What confronts us builds character and makes us into who we are to be. We are not our own. Once we come into that realization, we can begin to accept life's challenges and look at things entirely from a different perspective.

After experiencing so much racism and pain, you wonder why anyone would want to return to such a place. Love covers a multitude of sin, pain, and disappointment. Love draws, teaches, heals, and grows. What you see and experience makes you into what you don't want to do and who you don't want to become. The love in that three-room house and the wisdom and foundation I was built on gave me strength for my struggles beyond Alabama. If I had not endured Alabama's trials, I would not have survived Texas, the United Kingdom, Maryland, DC, and Illinois. Struggles and racism didn't just happen or stop in Alabama. Every place I have planted my feet on since leaving Alabama have taken me into another level of maturity and spiritual growth. Alabama's experiences were mild and a cakewalk in comparison to what I experienced after leaving. Alabama's hatred was blatant, open, and palpable, but the quiet, sneaky, underhand, and subtle hatred that I experienced in other places was more damaging. It reminded me of the deception of the cotton fields looking like snow. Once you get there and see what it looks like, you find that it is not as it appears. The grass is not always greener on the other side; it's just as deep and deceptive as where you're standing at the moment.

Chapter Two
Adulthood

After I finished school, I moved to Illinois. My sisters graduated the year before me and moved there, and I moved in with them. After they left home and would come back to visit, I was so excited to see them and couldn't wait until it was my time to leave. I graduated on Monday, and Tuesday, I was on a Greyhound bus headed to Illinois. When I got there, I thought, *Oh no, this is not what I thought it would be.* When I arrived at the bus station, it was dirty, and there were all types of people inside and outside, which I was not accustomed to seeing. They were homeless and unkempt and were begging. I was scared to death, to say the least. I wasn't used to what I was seeing. Alabama is known for its beauty and cleanness. As soon as I got there, I began looking for employment, and within a week, I had a job. The money was very good, considering where I came from, and that was my first job. The job was on the south side of Chicago, and I had to ride a subway train and transfer buses to get to the job. I liked what I was doing. I worked at Aldens, a mail ordering company. Getting there was my problem because I didn't like the subway and bus system. I began dreaming again about how I could get away from riding the train and bus to get to work. I had this vision again about becoming a model, and since I was in Chicago, maybe this was where I could look into getting my start as a model.

I was 6 feet 1 and 123 pounds. I was model material. One evening, coming home from work after getting off the last transfer bus, I was walking down the street near my apartment when a man walked up to me and asked for my name. He told me he had been noticing me as I passed his shop. He asked me if I would be interested in modeling for his shop because I had the right height and build for a model. You could have knocked me over. I was so excited. This was my dream, and here was a man right in my face talking to me about my dream. He told me he owned the boutique that I passed by daily and that the majority of the clothes in his boutique was made by him. I hadn't really noticed the shop. He gave me his business card and told me to call him and set up an appointment with him to discuss modeling some of the clothes in his shop.

I stopped by a few days later, and he told me he had some specific clothing he wanted me to model and asked me how I felt about being on *Soul Train*. *Soul Train* was a TV show that had well-known entertainers from the music industry, and there were dancers on the show as well. *Soul Train* was hosted by Don Cornelius at the time, and it was broadcast locally in Chicago until it went national. Nevertheless, I was ecstatic. I would appear on the show and wear the clothes from this boutique to dance in. I couldn't wait to get home and tell my sister Amie about it. I was going to be on television, and next, I was going to Paris. Paris was just my dream. He didn't mention anything like that, but if I could make it to television, I was sure Paris was next.

I did appear on *Soul Train* a couple of weeks later. I wore the clothes the owner of the boutique wanted seen on the show. I was a hit on *Soul Train*. I was to appear again on the show the following weekend, and he asked me if I could stop by his shop on a Sunday because he had made something specifically for me to wear on the show. I didn't think anything of this. Being gullible, naive, and excited about my adventure, I went to his shop on a Sunday. The shop was closed on Sundays, but he was there and let me in. He was there alone and started showing me what he wanted me to wear and the plans he had for me and how I could go far in the industry if I made the right connections. He told me being on *Soul Train* was a major step in that direction. I was so excited, and he was excited because I was excited. He handed me a couple of outfits and told me to go into the dressing room to try them on.

As I was undressing and most of my clothes were off, he entered the dressing room and attempted to rape me. Fortunately and thankfully, I was able to fight him off and was saved when another girl began banging on the door to get in. She was there to be fitted also. With the noise being made, he let go of me and went to open the door. I put my clothes back on and warned the young lady that was there what he had done. I left the shop and didn't know if she left or stayed. I was just thankful I escaped.

That ended my dream of becoming a model. I had signed a contract with the owner of this boutique, and he tried to sue me. I had to go to court to get out of it. After I explained to the judge why I wanted out of the contract, the case was dismissed. I didn't press charges against him. After that experience, I was through with modeling.

The weather started changing, and I could not handle the cold, so I began dreaming about leaving Chicago.

Marriage

Being married was something I always wanted. Unfortunately, I have been married three times. What I discovered about marriage has to do with wanting affection and to be loved by a male. I was raised in a home without a male figure being present. I never knew who my father was as a child. I desired affection and wanted to be loved by a man, and I thought marriage would provide that missing piece in my life.

I was engaged to my high school sweetheart when I finished school. We started dating when I was twelve years old, and I just knew he was to be my husband. Being raised in the South, marriage was prevalent. Once you finished school, you got married if you didn't attend college. When I graduated from high school, he was in the Air Force stationed in Okinawa, Japan, and I moved to Chicago. After Okinawa, his next assignment was Tacoma, Washington. Before going to this next duty station, he returned to Alabama on leave. I took a two-week vacation and joined him. Two months later, after I returned to Chicago, I discovered I was pregnant. I joined him months later in Washington State, where he and I got married. Our son Jerry was born there.

Being married at eighteen and pregnant was challenging. I was so far from home and didn't know the first thing about being a mother or wife. I didn't know how to boil water, so I made a lot of long-distance calls to Mutt Dear asking her how to cook certain things. I had a serious craving for gravy and biscuits when I was pregnant. I didn't know how to make either, so I called home. She tried to tell me how to make them, but that turned into a disaster, and what I made didn't taste like hers. I cried like a baby because I wanted gravy and biscuits and didn't know how to make them.

When I went into labor, I didn't know I was in labor. I didn't know what it felt like. I thought I had to use the bathroom, so I kept going to the bathroom and sitting on the toilet. I wasn't in pain. My stomach was just cramping. I realized I was in labor when my water broke while sitting on the toilet at home. My husband began experiencing pain, and he started throwing up. He went into labor. I never did. By the time I made it to the hospital, they took me directly into the delivery because the baby's head was partially showing and he would come right away. I was there less than an hour. I delivered a 9-pound, 2 1/2-ounce son. My husband was in the waiting area still throwing up and in pain. I was told that it was rare, but some men go into labor while the wives never feel a thing. Better him than me. I never had morning sickness. He did. After I had our son and the nurse gave him to me, I didn't know how to hold a baby. She made fun of that, and I cried because she was right. I didn't know how to hold my son. I wanted Mutt Dear, but she wasn't able to come because she couldn't afford it. To travel that far was very expensive.

I went through my pregnancy alone without my mom, and that was when I needed her the most, or so I thought. That experience taught me another lesson. It showed me how strong I was and that I had to learn to depend upon myself.

After I came home from the hospital, it was just my husband and I trying to take care of a newborn. Neither one of us had any experience in that department, but we learned together. I became upset with my mom, and depression set in after my son was born. My twin sisters who are older had children, and Mutt Dear was there for them. One of the twins was in New York, and the other was in Chicago. She had traveled there for them when they gave birth to their children, and that made me feel some type of way. I began looking at things in a different perspective and thought of her caring more for them than she did for me. I had always felt different when we were growing up and felt partiality from Mutt Dear compared with my siblings. Her not being with me when I had my baby made me think what I had suspected was true. There were five of us, but I felt that I was loved less. I had those thoughts because I did not have the same father as the others.

After moving to Maryland in the 80's I would go back to Alabama to visit, I spent all my time with my mom. During those times, she and I talked a lot and she shared many things with me—things about her childhood and adult life that she said she had never shared with anyone before. We both talked about our mistakes and how she raised us and the mistakes she made with us. Being an adult, I told her I understood and knew she did her best and what she thought was best at the time.

One of the things we discussed was how I thought she cared more for my siblings than she did for me. I don't know where the phrase "black sheep of the family" came from, but I felt that I was that sheep in our family. When a person feels that way, they have their own version of what a black sheep is or feels like. My version of a black sheep is being different, being the outcast, and feeling left out and alone all the time. As a child, those emotions put you in a place of insecurity and in a place one doesn't understand as a child. Becoming an adult, you still see that stigma of being the black sheep, so to speak. You look at the meaning in a different perspective, and it's now a good thing. Black sheep are unique, creative, and special in their own way. Being different is okay. It's how an individual looks at themselves that matters. We all are fearfully and wonderfully made and created with unique ways and gifts to make the world go around. If everyone was the same, the world would be boring, to say the least. It's about loving and accepting who you are.

Mutt Dear made me see what I wasn't able to see as a child. I have one child, and I could not understand this. I guess you would have to be a mother of more than one child to see or understand this.

She said, "As a mother with more than one child, you love your children the same, but it takes more attention, nurturing, and time with some more than others because none of your children are the same."

What takes more for one child may take less for another, and because I was different and had a strong personality, she knew that I would be able to take care of myself because I was more like her than any of the other children. Mutt Dear was a survivor and a very strong and determined woman. After she told me that, I guess you can say I stuck my chest out and took that as the greatest compliment ever. Even if she only told me that to make me feel good, it worked.

I look like my mom. I got my build and height from her. I was the tallest of my siblings, and I hated being tall. It made me feel different because I stand out from them. Mutt Dear taught me how to embrace my height, and I am so thankful she did. Because of my height, I would walk with my shoulders slumped inward to make myself look shorter, and that posture wasn't attractive. Whenever she saw me do this, she would tell me to stand up straight and threatened me that the next time she saw me walking that way, she would beat my butt. Well, she taught me, all right. One day, I was walking through the house, and out of nowhere, I felt a sharp pain across my shoulder. She hit me across the shoulder with an extension cord. She didn't have to say a word. I knew what it was for and why. From that day forward, I walked erect. What she said to me after that cord hit my shoulders remained with me.

After hitting me, she said to me, "One day, you will thank me."

In my mind, *I was thinking, How in the world will I thank you for hitting me with an extension cord?*

I thought she was crazy, but I knew better than to voice that. I sulked about her hitting me for a while, and one day, out of the blue, she said to me, "Shirley Jean, you're tall, and there is nothing you can do about that but like who you are and how you look. Wherever you go, you will be the first person that people will see because you stand above crowds, so when they look at you, give them something to look at. Walk like you own the world, walk straight with your head up, dress well, take care of yourself, and look good."

This was another well-taught lesson that carried me through society from the cotton fields to Capitol Hill.

Biological Father

Mutt Dear was married to my sibling's father. They were best friends and high school sweethearts While he was serving in the Armed Forces and stationed in Korea, she became involved with my father. When my stepfather returned from Korea, his homecoming was a surprise. No one was expecting his return on the day he arrived. When he showed up at home, Mutt Dear was sitting on the front porch in a chair, and when she looked up and saw him, she wouldn't move. When she did move and stood up, he saw her condition. She was seven months pregnant with me by someone else. She said the look and pain on his face said it all. He turned and walked away. He came back the next day to see my siblings, and after that, she did not see him again until he was leaving for his next duty station.

My mom and I talked about the hurt she caused him and the hurt he caused his children. Men are not as resilient as women. When women are hurt, we bounce back. We have to, especially when children are involved. We keep it moving. We have to because the majority of times, the sole responsibility of children falls upon the mother. Men can walk away from their responsibilities, their children, and everything and everyone involved when they are hurt. The hurt of a man goes deep, and for some unknown reason and understanding, they hold on to hurt longer and won't easily let go, forget, and forgive. Their hurt goes beyond the depth of the heart. It reaches and takes root in the mind, and the battle between the heart and the mind in a man becomes a powerful battle to fight and win. A man's heart takes precedence and overrules their mind. Pride can be the downfall of a man; they look at something as a sign of weakness when in reality it can be their strength. This is what makes women more resilient. We operate from the mind, and men operate from the heart. This is nothing that has been statistically proven. This is my own personal theory of a man's mind and a woman's heart.

This caused my mom and stepfather to divorce after he came home and saw her condition. Nothing was ever said to me directly, but I knew there was resentments toward me whenever my stepfather came around to visit my siblings. Action does speak louder than words. I felt that I was a reminder to him what took place between my dad and mom in his absence. I was twenty-five when he permanently came back into her life after their divorce. They remarried, but that didn't last long. They separated but remained living in close proximity of each other and spent most of their time together after separating. He was never far from her, even in her passing. He was there sitting by her bedside when she took her final breath. I was there as well, and I witnessed his love for her in her departure. Their love for each other was obvious and undeniable, but sometimes pain is hard to overcome even when love is deep.

Unfortunately, infidelity is a common and everyday action. There are consequences to every action or deed done, but when the consequences become vivid and undeniable, believing the fact is more painful than assuming or thinking or hearing the possibility of infidelity. People are more receptive to a lie than the truth. They would rather hear and be told a lie than see the evidence and witness truth.

The story with my mom and biological father is unconventional. Before I share their story, don't be so quick to judge. I share this story because I know many that have similar stories and, to this day, are in denial and are still keeping secrets about children conceived in infidelity.

We are not responsible for how we come into the world. Those that conceive and bring children into the world are accountable to God and not man, when what they do produces a child through and in their sin. My parents' relationship was based upon a physical attraction. Many of us have done something irresponsible at the spur of a moment and regretted afterward. It may not catch up with you immediately as it did my parents, but sooner or later, it has a way of knocking on your door.

"There is nothing hidden that shall not be revealed" (Luke 8:17), or you may haveheard it said this way: "What's done in the dark will come to the light." Pause for a second, and let that run through your mind. What have you done that you're living in fear of or waiting for the light to be turned on to expose your dark secrets and irresponsible behavior? I am the light that came on and shined on my parents' action. I am a product of their irresponsible behavior but a product with purpose. What the devil meant for evil God uses for His good. Babies or children are innocent in however they are conceived to come into this world. Whether rape, incest, or fulfilling the lust of the flesh, children are a blessing.

There is a blessing in everything that God allows to happen. We just have to see the blessing in what He allows. Did God allow two married people to commit adultery? No, it was their choice to do what they did. Was I the cause of my mom's and stepfather's divorce? No, I wasn't. There are consequences to sin, and divorce was the penalty my mom paid for her actions. Divorce wasn't a price my biological father paid because he remained married for fifty years until his wife's passing. This is the reason my mom never told me who my father was as a child. She said she didn't want to cause problems between my father and his wife. He kept his infidelity a secret from his wife. There was no substantial evidence in his part other than my mom's word saying that he was the father. There was no DNA test or anything at the time to prove who was the father of a child. It was only through the mother's verbal acknowledgment. I've heard many stories of children belonging to someone who wasn't their biological parent. No one wanted to tell the truth because of shame and embarrassment, remaining silent to keep peace.

Many men escaped being fathers to children they conceived because of hidden secrets or denial or they were trying to pass them on to someone else. The innocent, who is the child, should never view themselves as a mistake or accident or an embarrassment no matter the circumstance of their conception. Innocence is defined as blamelessness, not guilt. So what does that say of the guilty party?

My conception is interesting. I am here only because God ordained it so. My mom could have done what so many others do and have done. She could have aborted me. There wasn't any contraception during that time, or if there was, no one knew about it or could afford to purchase it.

My conception is no more a mistake than Jesus's conception was through Mary, His mother. God knew Mary would be Jesus's mother, and God knew Ester Lee would be my mother, however the conception. God had a purpose for Jesus, and He has a purpose for me. The way I was conceived was not designed by God, but He knew how I would be conceived before my parents knew they would do what they did. "'For I know the plans I have for you,' declares the LORD, 'plans to prosper you and not to harm you, plans to give you hope and a future'" (Jeremiah 29:11). With that being said and written before my world was formed, I have no shame in my conception.

I hope this will help someone who may be reading this and is struggling with their conception. For many years, I was ashamed of my conception, but my mother put it out there herself for those who knew her. When she made it public, I had no other choice but to accept and overcome my own shame. They knew about my conception before I was told, and no one ever told me the truth but my mother.

God knew this book would be written. He knew the contents and what the title would be before I was ever conceived. Nothing in life is by chance or coincidence. It's up to us to find the direction and get on that path. We will get on that path one way or another, either by choice or by force, but we will get there because we all are designed and created with purpose. Without us, God won't, and without Him, we can't. He needs us to operate through, to fulfill and complete His will and purpose. The one thing I love so much about God is how He will turn what appears to be the worst situation or scenario into a booming blessing.

My mom and some of her girlfriends in the cotton field noticed an attractive tall man. They made a bet with one another which of them could get him. What they meant by getting him neither of them considered the consequences or thought that getting him would go to the level it did. It started out as fun—just girls having fun, teasing one another, and flirting with this handsome man, even though they knew he was married and one of themselves was married as well. My mom's flirting went a little far, and the bet got out of hand. She won the billion-dollar flirting contest and *bam*! Yours truly was a result of that bet. I was conceived in a cotton field. Over half a century later, I am writing from the cotton field to Capitol Hill. When I began this journey of writing, this thought had never entered my mind—that literally my life, my conception, began in a cotton field. And here I am, telling the story.

What we go through in life and live through sometimes happens not to be kept a secret. What we go through can help others overcome their struggles when we share our stories. My mom and stepfather are deceased and my biological father is still living at the age of ninety-six, still tall, dark, and handsome and not looking his age but still trying to hold on to his secret about having what the world calls an outside child. In private, he acknowledges that I am his daughter, but in public, he avoids me and acts as if he is ashamed of me. I realize that it's not me he's ashamed of, but he's ashamed of himself and the guilt he has to live with. He has put himself in a position in life that made others think he had this perfect life and would do no wrong especially when adultery was concerned. Lies have a way of catching up with you regardless. All have sinned and fallen short of a perfect life.

Not long ago, I was in a doctor's office. There was a lady sitting across from me. She kept looking at me, and I was looking at her because she looked familiar, so we began talking. She asked me what church I attended and figured that this was probably where she had seen me. As I told her the name of my church, she told me the name of her church and said her husband was the pastor of the church she attended.

I said to her, "Oh yes, I know that church. My father attends your church."

She proceeded to ask who my father was, and I told her William Perkins. When I told her who my father was, she was appalled. She said to me, "Now that you said it, you look just like him. Wait until I tell my husband."

She told me that her husband was in the back, seeing the doctor. She hoped he would be finished before I left.

As luck would have it, her husband came out at that moment. She said to her husband, "Honey, who does this lady look like?"

He looked me over, and he said, "I don't know her, but she looks just like a Perkins."

His wife said to him, "This is Deacon Perkins's daughter."

He had to take a seat. He was so shocked. He said to me, "You look just like him and his sisters."

My dad's sisters attend his church as well. The pastor stated that my father had shared with him and the church in a testimony that he had been married for fifty years when his wife passed, and he had never been unfaithful to her in their marriage since her death. He said he had never been with another woman in his life. The pastor kept staring at me and said that just looking at me proved that my father had lied. My response to the pastor was "Lies have a way of catching up with you. What's done in the dark will come to the light."

Lives have been destroyed and families have been torn apart because of secrets. No one wants to tell the truth about what goes on in their family. I have heard stories of siblings unaware of each other and end up dating each other and having children together because of secrets. This could have happened between me and one of my brothers on my father's side if I had not known the truth. One of my brothers tried to date me. I am so thankful that my mom told me who my father was. If she had not told me, who knows what could have taken place in that situation? I told my brother he needed to talk with his father and come back and tell me what he said. He came back the next day. Apparently he didn't talk with him because he continued trying to get me to go out with him. I took it upon myself after that to go see our father. I knew where he worked, so I went to his job and told him he needed to talk with his son and tell him who I was because he was asking me out.

After that, I never saw him again, and when I did, he was distant with me. My father had four children, three of whom are older than myself—three boys and a girl. He shared with me that he had told them the truth of who I am to them. But the weirdest thing about it is that when they see me, they acted as if I have leprosy. They won't speak or come near me. Mary, my sister, doesn't hide her resentment toward me at all. I assumed from their actions he told them something. Maybe he told them the truth or maybe not. I spoke with a therapist about this and asked why their behavior toward me was resentful. She stated that for a girl, it's harder to accept. Being the only girl, if she was a daddy's girl, when someone comes into their space, jealousy and resentment will surface. Even if he didn't tell them the truth, others in his family knew the truth.

My father came from a large family, and they knew the truth of who I was. Before his mother passed, he took me to her house to meet her. It was strange how I met my grandmother. Again, this was literally a cotton-field experience. I was in the cotton field and very young. I couldn't have been no more than eight or nine. My dad was one of the Forman's of the cotton field. At lunch, this particular day, he came and took me from the field with one of his sisters, Annie Mae, and he took me up to their house. His mother was sitting on the porch in a chair with a blanket across her legs.

He said to his mom, "This is the little girl I was telling you about."

I remember her looking at me, and she gave me a hug and told me I was a pretty little girl. I didn't know or understand why he did that at the time. My mother wasn't with me in the field. It was only my siblings and me. After meeting his mom, Annie Mae took me back to the field where my siblings were, and I ate my lunch. I don't remember anything else about that event or if I even told Mutt Dear. I just remember meeting this little old lady that told me I was pretty.

Many people have left this world and have gone to their grave burying lies and secrets with them and left so much devastation behind because they were not truthful. Truth is power that can heal past and future generations of so much pain. I know a young lady who dated her brother and slept with him unknowingly. When they announced their engagement, her mom told her the boy she was dating was her half brother. Her mom was married, and the girl thought that the man her mom was married to was her biological father. The mother had an affair and had gotten pregnant while she was married and never told the husband or her daughter the truth. After the girl found out the truth, she tried to kill herself because she could not live with the fact that she had slept with her brother. This is why it is so important to tell the truth. You can live with the truth, but for someone to live with such a vile and sickening thought of sleeping with their brother or sister is horrid. Untruth is one of the biggest destroyers of life. Hidden secrets have caused mental, emotional, and physical damage to children and marriages, relationships, and families all in the name of status, reputation, shame, and guilt.

Unfortunately, since writing the story about my father, he passed away. His passing will forever be in my heart and mind.

The day of his demise, I was sitting in Sunday morning church service, and all of a sudden, I was overcome with a feeling of sadness and emptiness. I began to weep and my heart was hurting. I wasn't sure what I was feeling, but I sensed something was leaving my body. I knew my father was in hospice care and was transitioning; I was told this by a family member a couple of days before.

After I got out of church, I called my dad's house and ask to speak with my sister Mary or brother Londa.

Londa replied, "This is Londa."

I told him who I was and asked if I could come over to see my dad.

He stated he didn't think it was a good idea, and no, I could not come over.

I said to him I just wanted to see him.

He said he wasn't being ugly, but I could not come.

After hanging up from him, I had a peace to come over me.

That same night at 9:00 p.m., I received a call from the same relative who told me he was in hospice care, telling me that he had passed. I didn't shed a tear when hearing this. I believe what I was feeling in church was my spirit connecting with my father, and in the spirit, he was saying goodbye to me. I didn't attend his funeral but struggled strongly about whether to attend or not. I thought if I was denied seeing him before his passing, I might receive the same treatment at his funeral from my siblings, so I stayed away.

Call Into Ministry

Before I was formed in my mother's womb, I was already called to minister, teach, and carry the Word of God. In the book of Jeremiah in the Bible, God told Jeremiah, "I knew you when you were in your mother's womb." The first day of our life begins with the purpose and destiny we were created for. From creation, I was special in God's sight, and the enemy knew this as well. He tried to kill me at birth, but God had other plans.

I was born at home and delivered by a midwife. Shortly after my birth, as I was lying in bed beside my mother, she happened to look over at me while I was covered in blood. My umbilical cord had come untied. I would have bled to death if she had not looked at me in time. Big Mama was there to retie the cord.

Another near-death experience happened when I was in my twenties. I was admitted to the hospital because I was losing weight and having blackouts. Several tests were done to me. In one particular test that was done, I had a reaction to the chemical that was injected into me, and my heart stopped beating. The hospital called a code blue on me. There's no formal definition for a code blue, but doctors often use the term as a slang for a cardiopulmonary arrest happening to a patient in a hospital or clinic, requiring a team of providers (sometimes called a code team) to rush to the specific location and begin immediate resuscitative efforts. As this code was called on me, I could hear what was taking place around me. I could hear the sound of running feet from the doctors and nurses. When I was hearing all of this, I had a vision of being in a tunnel, floating and surrounded by the most beautiful and brightest colors I have ever seen. I experienced a peace that I have never experienced before. I continued traveling through the tunnel and toward a bright light that was at the end of the tunnel. The closer I got to the end, the light became more extensive, and the colors were brighter all around me. These were colors that I had never seen before or since. They were indescribable—not the typical blue, pink, yellow, or green colors you see in crayon boxes. There was something to these colors that I can't describe or compare. When I think about it or try to describe them, all I can say is they were colors of glory. How is glory described, or what does it look like? There are no words for it, but the best description I have ever been able to give for the colors I saw is glorious.

I could hear conversation from the team that was working on me. I could still hear the doctors talking about my heart rate and how my heart had stopped. I heard one of them repeating over and over, "We are losing her. We're losing her." Once I heard that, I spoke to God in my spirit and said, "Not now, God." What about Jerry? Jerry is my son. He was a baby, and I didn't want to leave him. As soon as I said that, I began floating back upward to the opening of the tunnel. Instantly I heard and felt a sound in my heart, and one of the doctors said, "We have a beat."

When God has a plan for you, the devil in hell can't touch you. He can't take your life. Life and death are God's, and until you have completed and fulfilled His assignment for your life, death has no dominion over you. It's not over until God says it's over.

Did I want this call to minister? Does anyone want it? I can only speak for myself, and the answer was no. Obedience is better than sacrifice, and I accepted the call to minister. Does answering the call make life easier? No, it doesn't, but people have this misconception that it does. But it doesn't.

My first experience being called into ministry, I was lying in bed. What I experienced was surreal. "The natural man receives not the things of the spirit of God, for they are foolishness unto him; neither can he know them because they are spiritually discerned" (1 Corinthians 2:14). The Spirit carried me in a vision, and what I saw wasn't a natural dream but a spiritual dream. Dreams will sometimes make you question if they are real or if there is something else taking place. A vision is when you see something and you get a heavenly perspective either in your literal eyes or in your spiritual mind's eyes. A dream is what you see when you're asleep. Visions are clearer and less ambiguous in meaning than their dream counterparts. I had a vision. What I saw was in the spirit realm with my spiritual mind's eyes, and it was so real.

I was standing in the front door of my living room, with the door open. There was a tree in the front yard that stood at the right side of the house. The wind was blowing, and the tree was making a rustling sound. Its leaves were blowing from side to side. I looked up at the top of the tree, and there was a cloud hovering over the tree that looked as if it was just sitting on top of the branches. The clouds were clear blue with a bright crystal light shining directly through the leaves. The cloud began to expand and cover the entire front yard, and all of a sudden, the clouds started moving toward me. It came closer and closer, and the closer it got, an image began to take form in the cloud. As it continued moving toward me, I recognized the image as the image of Christ. In the image, there was a man in a robe, and under the robe, the image of arms and hands stretched out toward me. His feet were crossed as the image of the cross. No,

I did not see a face, only an image. I know that just ran across your mind as you read this.

As the image got closer, I said, "Tell me what you want me to do."

After I spoke this, I was drawn back into the natural realm, and the image disappeared, but the front of my yard was the exact image that was in my dream, made me question if what took place was an actual reality.

The next couple of days and weeks, I kept praying for this vision to return. I began searching my Bible to see if there were any biblical stories of anyone ever seeing an image like that or having a similar vision. Each time I picked up the Bible to read, as I opened it, the book is automatically opened up to the same page, passage, and scripture. That scripture confirmed what I knew in my spirit. That scripture stayed with me for twenty-five years, and twenty-five years later, each time I would open up the Bible and ask God to speak to me, it would fall open to the same page, passage, and scripture. Many years later, while studying the Bible, I read the book of Ezekiel and could relate to Ezekiel's experience with what I saw in my vision.

As a child, I was different and had phenomenal dreams and visions. I experienced things that I never told anyone about. I saw things that were unexplainable and was too afraid and ashamed to talk about them because either no one would believe me or they would think I was insane. When I was a little girl living in our three-bedroom house, I slept with Big Mama because of the lack of space. When I would go to bed at night, I would see things or feel something pulling the covers off me. I would sleep with the covers over my head and get very close to Big Mama because I was scared. Sometimes I would wake up screaming, but no sound would come out of my mouth. I knew I was screaming to the top of my lungs.

I did share once with Big Mama what was happening, but what she told me frightened me all the more, so I never mentioned it again. She said that it was witches riding me. I had no idea what that meant, and I didn't want to know because when she mentioned witches, I knew whatever that was didn't sound good. Early 80's I lived in San Antonio, I witnessed many supernatural entities. I can say for sure those were not visions or dreams but actual events. Not only did I witness them, but my son and my second husband at the time witnessed them also.

In the 70's I was pregnant with my son, I lived in Tacoma, Washington. I had this constant dream and saw the same image. Each night, when I went to bed, there was an image of a dark shadow that would come out of the closet. My bed faced the closet door, and I would always sleep on my right side, facing the closet. Each night and early in the morning, I felt something approaching me. It didn't seem like a dream, and I would be awakened. This shadow always tried to reach out and touch my stomach, but before it got close enough to touch me, I would tell myself it was just a dream and then wake myself up. Whatever this was followed my son up until he was an adult. I believe up to now, that which was disturbing, my spirit was me being equipped and prepared for the call of ministry, not only for me but my son who is also in ministry and pastor a church. My son is now grown, and has a son of his own. The same thing has happened with his son who I feel have the same call for his life to minister.

When I lived in San Antonio, one night, as we were all asleep, I was awakened by a scream coming from my son's bedroom. He said, "Mama, a man is standing in my door."

My husband and I both jumped up, and as we reached his room, we both saw a dark shadow of a man standing in the door of his room. My husband went for his gun, but I told him, "This wasn't something you would kill with a gun."

This shadow began moving away from us—down the hall, away from my son's bedroom door, and toward the garage, fading as it walked through the kitchen and disappeared.

A few days later, my husband and I were lying in bed, talking in the dark. I can't remember if we were talking about what had happened with my son or what exactly the conversation was about, but I remembered saying to him God is going to get you because of what he was saying to me. All of a sudden, in the corner of the bedroom, a bright light lit up the room. The light was so bright, and as I looked to see what it was, there stood in the corner a burning bush. It was on fire. I didn't feel fear at all. I felt a calmness, and I asked my husband if he could see it. He did. And just then, it disappeared as fast as it had appeared, but we both saw it. We didn't talk about what had taken place that night as we were getting ready for work the next morning because my son was getting dressed for school and we didn't want to frighten him. I thought of the story of Moses in the Bible, when he went up into the mountains and God appeared to him through a burning bush. Maybe that was why it didn't frighten me.

When we went to work the next day, he called me for lunch and wanted to go back to the house. We went back to the house, and by then, we both were a little fearful. We didn't know what to expect, but we went in and walked through the house. As we walked through the house, it seemed okay at first. We ate lunch and was about to leave to go back to work. We were in the bathrooms where there were two joining bathrooms to our bedroom. The door was opened to the other bathroom he was in. I was brushing my teeth, and we could see each other.

He said, "I think what was here last night is gone."

And as soon as he said that, a force of wind very strong swept past us. We could feel the presence of something, but we couldn't see it. The presence was so powerful it nearly knocked me down. We both left and went back to work, and that time, I was scared. After work, we came home and prayed over the house and anointed it with oil, but we never shared this with my son because I knew it would frighten him even more.

The incident that happened to my son, which was the shadow of a man, happened a lot when we lived in Alabama, prior to moving to Texas. He always wanted to sleep with me, but I wouldn't let him because if I let him sleep with me, he would get in a habit and not want to sleep in his own bed. When I wouldn't let him sleep with me, I would find him asleep on the floor at the foot of my bed or next to me on the floor beside the bed when I wake up the next morning. He would tell me that he saw the man again and that he was trying to get him. I didn't put all this together until I became older and became more in touch with my spirituality. I realized now that it was part of my spiritual growth and preparation for ministry. Spirits are real, and many people don't believe and realize that they are.

Moses spent forty years in the wilderness as God equipped and prepared him for the call. I spent twenty-five years in my wilderness to be equipped. We are the tool and vessel that makes the world operate. We are not the creator of the world, but our Creator uses us to get things done. So many people today feel they have no purpose in life and that their lives are worthless. Once we come into the knowledge and acceptance that we are not our own and that we have purpose, not just ourselves to be concerned about, we will be better off and live happier lives. We are put here to help meet the needs of others. In doing this, we see and feel self-worth and value. God wants and needs us just as much as we want and need Him. The trials of life are character builders for the purpose of God's use. Life is not about us but about God. We can avoid many bumps and bruises of life when we come to this realization.

Every phase of life has not been about me; it's about what and where God was taking me to get me where I am today. Wherever you are and whatever you are doing, you are operating in the now fulfilling God's purpose until your demise. We didn't just enter into the world on the day that we were born through physical birth from woman, but we are also in the beginning manifested into the now for God's plans only. That goes for all of us. We get so absorbed in ourselves and what we think and want that we forget that life's purpose is not about us; it's about fulfilling the will of God on earth as it is in heaven. Sometimes what we go through does make us forget about others. When the burden and pain are so enormous, all you can think about is yourself. Even through that, God gets the glory because each circumstance takes you higher into your relationship with Him.

I've heard people say, "New level, new devil." I beg to differ: new level, greater glory. We become greater witnesses of Christ for those who will experience what you have gone through. We all have been given a measure of faith—some stronger than others. We can sometimes go through the same situation, but it is according to your faith how you go through and come out.

When you look back over your lives, what can you say about yourself? When we survey and analyze what we have gone through and experienced, do you ask yourself if it had to take all that to get to where you are today? What we go through in life is a process to make us who we are today. Each experience is a learning and growing process. You can't grow if you stand still in the same position. There is lot to analyze and dissect. There are many questions we ask ourselves. What did you learn, and what would you do differently? Where do you go from that point?

What does it actually mean when we say, "Hindsight is twenty-twenty?" It's easy to know the right thing to do or say afterward because you can't predict the future. Hindsight is knowing the facts about things after they've happened. Life is not twenty-twenty. Twenty-twenty is perfect vision, and no one is perfect; therefore, mistakes will be made. This means that you didn't think that what took place in the past was right, but now that you think back on it, you realize that it was right after all. Retrospectively, you can easily tell what you should have, could have, and would have done. Never worry over spilled milk; you can't put it back into the bottle. You can't go back and undo what's been done. There is nothing you can do about the past, but let the past be just what it is and keep it moving. Don't worry over past choices and decisions because you can't change one thing about them. Let it be a learning lesson. When you know better, you do better.

People have a tendency to blame others like their parents for things that didn't go well for them. I was guilty of that. I blamed my mom for a lot of things, but as I became a parent, my son blames me for a lot of things as well. Yes, I did not make the best decisions, but at that particular time, I made what I thought was the best decision. We find ourselves saying, "When I have children, I won't do what my parents did to me," but as we mature, we can see and understand why they did what they did. We never have all the answers. Experience is the best teacher in the world. Experiences give and reveal answers.

The cotton field was the setup that qualified and equipped me for my twenty-five-year wilderness. The heat, agony, and back pain was brutal, but in comparison to life afterward, the cotton fields were a cakewalk. Moses was in his waiting period of forty years before delivering the children of Israel out of Egypt. He grew in wisdom and faith. Experiences developed his intimate relationship with God. My wilderness experience taught me the same lessons. My twenty-five years were a life-changing journey of good, better, and best.

I read a quote by St. Jerome Brainy that says, "Never let it rest until your good is better and your better is best." Good began in the day of conception. Better precedes conception, and best supersedes all that's in between.

In Job 8:7, God promised Job that his latter would be greater. It says though thy beginning was small, the latter end should greatly increase. I can say I am a living witness to this promise. God is no respecter of persons; what He does for others He will do the same for you when you believe. I am living the best days of my life. My latter is greater. Just as He promised Job, He has offered us that same promise. He is the same today, yesterday, and forever. He never changes.

Initial Sermon

I was called to minister in Alabama, but I didn't deliver my initial message until many years later in Washington, DC, under the leadership of Bishop Michael V. Kelsey at the New Samaritan Baptist Church. My initial message came from John 15:16—"You have not chosen me, but I have chosen you and ordained you that you should go and bring forth fruit and that your fruit should remain that whatsoever you ask of the Father in my name I will give it to you." This was the passage, verse, and scripture that followed me for twenty-five years until December 19, 2001, after I saw the vision standing in my door of my apartment.

Two years before, I was allowed to enter a pulpit and deliver my first message. It was mandatory to be in MIT (minister in training) for those years. I attended seminary school and took several classes before I was ever considered to be licensed as a minister. Unfortunately, this form of training doesn't apply everywhere and to everyone today. The North and South have different views about who can and cannot be licensed as ministers. Women are not accepted in ministry in many churches in the South. Nelson Mandela quoted these words about gender equality: "Freedom cannot be achieved unless women have been emancipated from all forms of oppression."

People are held hostage and kept in bondage by race, gender, and status because of man-made rules. I look forward to the day that we are delivered from ignorance of all form. It is my prayer that this twenty-first century, particularly the Southern Baptist Church, would be delivered from the slavery mentality about a woman's place and position in society and would stop following manmade rules about women in ministry and allow them to do what God has ordained, appointed, and anointed them to do. I also know that this was God's plan for me—to be licensed in the North—because I would not have been licensed in the South at the church I was attending because the South opposes women in ministry.

We focused upon the wrong things and this is one reason we are losing generations. We are more interested in the things of the world than saving souls. Because Christianity is not taken seriously and not operating on faith based on the Word of God, our churches are becoming empty and souls are being lost to the world. If a male says they have been called into ministry, no question is asked nor is there a waiting period. They are put in the pulpit immediately, given the title licensed, and allowed to operate in the position just by their word alone. Some are called, and some have called themselves, but they are accepted just because of gender. I could defend the rejection of women being in the pulpit all day, but that battle is not mine to fight. It's already been fought and won, and man has to answer to God for going against His Word and will to appease manmade rules just to be a part of the good-old boy club. Women who have been called are ordained by God. I was ordained, anointed, and appointed by God when I was conceived in sin. And who is man to say who I am? I am who I am as God has called me.

The first message in the Bible after the resurrection of Christ was given to a woman by Jesus Himself to be delivered to others. God says He is no respecter of persons. There is neither Jew nor Greek. There is neither bond nor free. There is neither male nor female, for we are all one in Christ Jesus (Roman: 3:28). Who can argue against that?

I appreciate the training and the waiting I received. I appreciate the wilderness experiences that I went through prior to my initial message. When someone is genuine in their call through the message and in their deliverance of that message, the authenticity will be seen, felt, and heard. Once the world learns that man cannot stop what God ordains, the world will be a better place.

Living Abroad

In the 80's I had the opportunity to travel abroad after becoming married for the second time to someone who was in the military. The direction that life will take you to fulfill a dream or desire is amazing. My cotton-field fantasy of going abroad did transpire, but not in the way that I hoped or imagined. I didn't become the model I dreamed of, but the opportunity was there. I was in London, sightseeing and shopping at Harrods. If you've even been to London, you know it's one of the most exquisite and fashionable places in the UK. As I was browsing through some of the shops, I was approached by a designer who was there in one of the stores. He asked me if I had ever modeled and if I would be interested in showcasing some of their designs. Being six feet one, I was noticeable as mom told me when I got the cord across my back. And I must say I wasn't hard on the eye either. I was given a business card and told that if I was interested, I could contact him. How ironic is this story to what happened in Chicago? I was being offered to model a second time.

If I had only known my dream of going overseas was going to be a living nightmare. That was one dream I would have asked God to remove as one of my heart's desires. Psalm 37:4 tells us to delight ourselves in the Lord and He will give us the desires of our heart. Before getting married a second time, I was in a relationship with my second husband for seven years and had no idea that he was abusive, physically and mentally. To say that you never know a person until you live with them is a fact. I married a nightmare from hell, and that nightmare of a husband disapproved of me pursuing modeling, so that ended my dream there.

Being a military dependent overseas, you basically are limited to what you can and cannot do. The person who is your sponsor, as well as your husband or wife, is responsible for your actions as a dependent internationally. My husband knew this, and he took it to the extreme and used his authority to mentally and physically abuse me. The military covered up his behavior because of who he worked for and where. He was in the Air Force, and he worked as JAG (judge advocate general). I reported his abuse, but nothing was ever done to assist me. Being physically and mentally abused, I made several trips to the base hospital. The worst visit to the hospital was when I was nearly choked to death. One of the doctors thought that a bone in my throat was broken. To determine if it was broken, a tube was put through my nose, and it was run through my chest for an x-ray. I had to be awake for this to be done, and I was by myself. There was one particular doctor who noticed that I had made several trips to the ER after reviewing my medical records and seeing how often I was in and out of the ER. Each time I went to the ER, I would make up excuses to cover up the abuse. The doctor who saw me the last time was a colonel, and he asked me if I was being abused. When he asked me that question, my mind and body exploded. I burst into uncontrollable tears that I thought would never stop. After what seemed like hours of crying and being emptied of what I had kept locked up inside, finally I got myself together. I opened up to the colonel and told him everything I had been going through. He told me that he would help me and would report this to the base commander. I gave him my husband's information, and he promised me that would be my last visit to the hospital for that reason. I thought, *Finally, someone is going to help me.* But that never happened. I never knew what happened or if the colonel reported the abuse. I had gone to the base security police a couple of times and filed a report for abuse, and nothing became of that either.

Every complaint reported on the base went through the JAG. The JAG is the office that serves as legal advisors to the commander and addresses base complaints. Because my husband worked at the JAG, I knew this was why nothing was ever done to help me. I don't know if the reports ever reached the appropriate desk or person because he would destroy the report before they could be given to the right person because nothing was done. One day, I went into the JAG when I knew Johnny, my husband, was out of the office. I went there and asked to speak with his commanding officer. I explained the situation to him and told him what was going on. I asked about the report that I filed with security police. I asked if a report from the hospital had ever been filed. I was told that my complaints would be looked into and that they would get back with me. Once again, no one ever got back with me.

I endured his abuse for four years. That was how long his assignment lasted. Someone asked me once why I didn't leave and return to the US. I couldn't because he had taken my passport and I could never find it. I had to go through the JAG to get a replacement, and that was a no-no since he worked there.

I survived those four years only by the grace and mercy of God because the military wasn't of any help. It was evident that they were more concerned with protecting the reputation of the office and military personnel and their reputation than that of a dependent. The mental abuse I was subjected to was worse than the physical abuse. There was one particular incident at the ER that was so traumatic. My mental state was in such jeopardy that when they asked for my name, I couldn't remember it. I was in a place of such darkness in my mind. If anyone had touched me, I would have fallen completely over the edge and never returned mentally.

The embarrassment and pain of being mentally and physically abused and feeling helpless because no one was there to help were so immense I couldn't see any way out but to go to this place of darkness in my mind where there was this black hole that seemed to be waiting to hide and cover my pain. That made me forget what I was going through. I couldn't remember my name because my mind was telling me if I forget who I was, everything would go away, especially the pain. I remember fighting with everything in me not to fall over the edge into total darkness. There was a war going on inside my head. I was in a battle with sanity and insanity. Another part of my mind was reminding me that there was something I could and should do, but I couldn't remember what that was. I kept looking at the black hole that was pulling me in the wrong direction. The battle taking place in my head was between my mind and soul. Something inside me was fighting to remind me what that something was. In place of saying my name, I began repeating the twenty-third Psalm. Prayer—that was the something I was supposed to do, and that was the something that kept my sanity and kept me from going totally into the abyss of darkness. It was God's grace that keep my sanity.

The battle that was taking place was of the spirits of light and darkness, good and evil. Now I realize that it was spiritual warfare. I could have chosen darkness and gone into that dark hole, which was the devil himself trying to take my mind. This incident reminded me of my near-death experience in the hospital, being in the tunnel when a code blue was called on me in Alabama. Again, this incident demonstrates that life and death can be a choice. Not in all instances are we given the choice to live or die. Life and death are in the power of God, but sometimes God allows us to make the choice to live or die. I chose to live.

I began reciting the twenty-third Psalm. I could not remember all of it. I only remembered "The Lord is my shepherd," and I continued repeating over and over, "The Lord is my shepherd." All at once, it came back to my memory: "The Lord is my shepherd; I shall not want. He makes me to lie down in green pastures. He leads me beside the still waters. He restores my soul. He leads me in the paths of righteousness for his name's sake. Yea, though I walk through the valley of the shadow of death, I will fear no evil, for thou *art* with me. Thy rod and thy staff they comfort me. Thou prepare a table before me in the presence of mine enemies. Thou anoint my head with oil; my cup runneth over. Surely goodness and mercy shall follow me all the days of my life. And I will dwell in the house of the LORD forever."

"And I will dwell in the house of the Lord"—those are the words that resonated so strongly when I spoke them. Instantly it was as if I was lifted off the bed I was lying on. When I spoke those words, I knew that I was in the presence of God and that He was with me. I felt the darkness lifting off and being replaced with peace. It was a peace so overwhelming that it came upon me and into my mind and magnified my name. It was so joyful that I spoke my name with such power and vigor, and it frightened the doctor attending me. I guess he may have thought that

I had really lost my mind at that point. I kept saying my name over and over. I still love saying my name, and I love the sound of it because I remember when I couldn't remember how to say it. Saying my name reminds me of who I am, where I am, and how the Lord kept me from going into an abyss and losing who Shirley is. I researched the name Shirley many years ago. It says the name creates an active mind, a restless urge to explore new ideas, and self-confidence, and my favorite expression is "I know." I thought to myself how interesting it was because much of this is me—it is Shirley.

When I think about that day now, it makes me think of my mother. She died of Alzheimer's disease. I was living in Maryland when she became sick. When I would come home to visit her, she would stare at me and keep asking me my name. I so proudly but softly would tell her my name, and a few minutes later, she would repeat and say, "Now who did you say you are?" or ask "Who are you?"

If you have ever been around anyone with Alzheimer's disease, you know that they repeat themselves over and over. When I would look into her eyes, it was like looking into a dark empty hole. I used to wonder if somewhere in the dark hole of her mind she knew who I was but just couldn't call out my name. I would think to myself, *I am your baby. How could you not know me?* I wanted her to come back to me so badly that I told myself that she could choose to come back from that place of darkness if she wanted too. Looking into her eyes and seeing darkness and emptiness made me wonder where her mind was. Was there some emotional pain or hurt that had pushed her into forgetting and not wanting to remember who she was just as I nearly did? I didn't think about what she had as a sickness because of what I had been through emotionally and found the will and strength to come out of. Maybe I was in denial and didn't want to accept what was happening to her.

I hoped she could see in my eyes how much I wanted her to return and remember me.

I sent my son back to the States to live with his father. Not only was the abuse taking a toll on me but it was affecting my son. I received a call from his school one day, telling me he was having problems focusing in class and that he was falling asleep on his desk. I knew it was because of the arguing and fighting that were going on at home all through the night. I began to notice the mental abuse being directed toward my son, and I knew something had to be done. The only thing I could think of was to send him back to the States to his father. I didn't realize how he was mentally abusing my son until one day when I came home early from work and he had my son cut grass with a hand held push mower in the rain. The four years I was in England, it seemed like it rained nonstop twenty four seven, all year round.

My son was pushing the mower and crying, with his clothes soaked from the rain. I had him stop and come inside, away from the rain. My husband and I got into a fight over that. He said my son was lazy and that he was trying to make a man out of him. I was so angry at that point I wanted to murder him. He drank a lot, and he had been drinking when that happened. After things had calmed down, he fell asleep on the sofa. I was still upset about what he had my son do in the rain. He was eleven years old at the time. While he was sleeping, I kept watching him, still seeing the hurt in my baby's eyes as he was pushing and cutting grass in the rain. The more I looked at him lying on the couch, the angrier I became.

I thought, *I can take his abuse, but he cannot inflict that upon my child.*

As I was standing over him, all kinds of thoughts were running through my mind. *What had he done to my son, or what could he have done to him when I wasn't around?*

I went into the kitchen to get a butcher knife, and I thought, *No, that wouldn't be good enough for him.*

If I had had a gun, I knew I would have shot him. Guns were not allowed in a foreign country, so that saved his butt from me shooting him. The next thing that entered my mind, I looked beneath the kitchen sink and got a can of charcoal lighter fluid. I walked back into the living room and poured it on him. He had been drinking, so he didn't hear, feel, or smell the liquid and never woke up. I had a cigarette lighter in my hand, and I was going to set him on fire.

I thought that my son was in his room, but he came up behind me from out of nowhere—so it seemed—and he yelled, "Mama, no!"

I had not given any thought to the consequences of what I was about to do. If I had set that fool on fire, the whole house could have burned down, and this being government property, I would have been in double trouble. I didn't care at the moment. I wanted to kill him because of the pain I saw in my baby's face when he came in from the rain. The tone and sound of my son's voice when he yelled "Mama, no" was the only thing that saved him and kept me from grilling his butt. The fool never woke up, and he never said anything about why he smelled like lighter fluid or why his clothes were wet. I guess the alcohol made him think his mind had played tricks on him, so he couldn't remember what had happened. If I had set him on fire, I would have gone to prison in Europe and probably would have never been able to return to the US. I knew then I had to do something to get my son out of that situation, so I sent him home. I had my son's passport, and I told my husband I was going to send him home to live with his father. I didn't get any backlash from that, so I sent him back to live with his father.

Going through all of this, I never told anyone. I kept this from my family, especially Mutt Dear. She tried to get me not to marry him, but I didn't listen. When I called home, which was seldom because it was so expensive to make international calls doing that time, I pretended everything was good. One of the things women in abusive relationships do is keep secrets and put up a front. There was only one person who knew what I was going through at the time. She was a military dependent as well, and she was going through something similar. She and I became very good friends and still remain friends to this day. She was much younger than me, and we connected and developed a very close bond. We strengthened and encouraged each other. We lived close to each other in base housing. She had three small children. My son would babysit her children at times. Her husband and mine were friends as well; they were drinking buddies, as they called each other. There was a lot of abuse taking place on base, but no one talked about it.

We were living in base housing on Upper Heyford Air Force Base in England. The houses were connected and very close. The walls were thin, and I could hear the abuse from the couple next door. I am sure she could hear mine as well. I never connected with the woman next door. We only spoke in passing as I would see her going in and out. The look she had about her was the look that I was so familiar with. That was the look of abuse. When you've been through mental or physical abuse, you unknowingly take on a look of what you are being subjected to. I know the look and can identify it whenever I see it to this day. Thank God I no longer wear that look and don't look like what I've been through.

I was one of those women who said I would never allow certain things to be done to me by a man, and I thought I knew what I would or wouldn't do if they did. Having been in that position, I understand why some women stay in their situation. Situations and circumstances are different. Some stay, and some leave. I stayed because at the time I had no other place to go to, being so far from home. I knew that once I got back to the US and set foot on American soil, things would change for me. I had my son to provide for and protect, but after sending him back home, it was just me. I could take care of myself even if it meant living on the streets. And that was exactly what happened next.

Transitioning Back To The U.S.

At the end of his four-year term mid 80's being stationed in the UK, we got orders to return to the US. We were stationed in the Washington, DC, Bolling Air Force Base. I loved the UK, and in a somewhat confusing and strange way, I was sad to leave. It was the country and the beauty of it that I would miss, but I wanted to get back to the US because I knew I would be getting out of the abuse I had endured for four years. Before Permanent Change of Station's from Upper Heyford Air Force Base to return home, there were certain procedures you had to go through. Dependents lose a lot of their independence to their spouses when they are stationed internationally. One of the things dependents were entitled to was that their spouse wasn't privy to their medical records. During my processing, I went to the hospital to get my medical records, only to find that they were picked up by my husband. Someone had violated a federal rule and given him my records, but because he worked at the JAG, there were certain rules again that didn't apply. My medical records were the evidence that I needed and was going to use to prove the physical abuse that I had endured for four years when I file for divorce. After the divorce, I had planned to go back to Alabama, but I had to go to DC first because that's where all my household goods were being shipped. It would be a while before they arrived to the States.

When I got to DC, it was one of the worst months of the year. It was February, and *cold* wasn't the word. I've never liked cold weather, but cold or not, I was happy to be back on American soil. We lived in base housing for two weeks and began looking for a place to live. Within a week, he found a place in Fort Washington, Maryland. Things were going well. The household goods shipment arrived sooner than I thought, and we settled into the house. After getting settled, it wasn't a week before the abuse started. This time, I ended up with a broken wrist.

When my wrist was broken, I didn't realize it was broken right away. I went to work the next day, and halfway through the day, my wrist began hurting so badly I couldn't lift a pencil. After I got off work and was on my way home, I decided to stop by the infirmary. After an x-ray was done, it was discovered that my wrist was fractured, and I had to wear a cast. I went home, and when I walked into the house, he asked me what happened to my wrist as if he didn't know the day before that he had abused me. I told him he broke my wrist, and he approached me and began his verbal abuse and denying that he was the cause of me being in a cast. And the abuse started again. I was trying to protect my wrist from further pain, so I ran from the house and was gone until I thought he had gone to bed, but when I returned, he wasn't there.

One of the things that some men do when they are being physically abusive is buy gifts after they abuse you. After that incident, he began his strategy of giving gifts again. I received diamonds, a fur coat, flowers, you name it—he bought them all for me. For years, he bought me gifts after he abused me. It took me a minute to realize what he was actually doing. After breaking my wrist, he turned on his charm and took it to another level. But this time, I wasn't falling for anything he did or said.

I was on American soil, and this time, I knew someone would listen to me.

I dated this man for seven years before marrying him, and I never saw that side of him. I asked myself a million times, "How did I miss those signs?" I never saw them, and the abuse never started until I moved to Texas with him and said "I do." We were in a long-distance relationship all those years, and when we saw each other, it was excitement because of the absence. Absence does makes the heart grow fonder. He was very clever and was a master at hiding his realness. I didn't see that because his charm swept me off my feet.

After returning home and seeing he wasn't there after the attack, I called a relative who lived in Maryland. She and her husband came to pick me up. One look at me and they took me to the ER on Andrews Air Force Base. With my wrist being in a cast and with bruises on my body, a doctor at the hospital began questioning me. I told him what I had been through the past four years and how I reported it and nothing was done while I was stationed in England. He didn't say anything after talking and then examined me. I sat in the exam room nearly an hour. The next thing I knew, two non-commission officer enlisted personnel came into the room and informed me they couldn't locate my medical records. They told me that they would keep me overnight, but the next day, I would be given temporary living quarters on base and didn't have to return home.

I stayed in temporary quarters for seven days. I had no idea what was taking place. A week later, there was a knock at the door. As I opened the door, there, standing in front of me, were two uniformed military officers telling me that I could return home and that my husband had been discharged from the military. I thought, *I can't go back to the house especially since he had lost his job.* I knew this time he would kill me. I was told by the military that I could call the civilian police and they would accompany me back to my home to get some of my clothes. I took a taxi back to the house from the base. My husband was there, and so were the Maryland police. They let me go inside to get some clothes. I could only take so much, so I took one of the cars and put the few things in the car that I was able to take with me.

I slept in my car in the parking lot of a supermarket on Old Fort Road that night. I went to work the next day at the Pentagon. That was my first day back after being off a week. When I got off work, I went out to the place I normally parked my car but couldn't find it. I went back inside to report my missing car. It took a while, but the Pentagon security camera that overlooked the parking lots saw that my car was taken by my husband. He knew where I parked daily. So there I was, without a car, and the few clothes I had in the car were gone. I called my neighbor, and she told me that a moving van came that morning and moved everything out, and the house was empty. I needed to get home, so I went to an ATM inside the Pentagon to take out some cash, only to find out all that was left in the account was five dollars. He had taken all the money out—both saving and checking accounts. I had a few dollars in my purse, and I did make it to the house on the subway and transfer buses into Fort Washington.

I needed to go to the house to see if he had left anything of mine, and unfortunately, he did not. Also, he changed the locks on the door, so I was unable to get into the house. I had no idea where he had gone. He had taken all my clothes, the furniture, both cars, and left me with nothing but the clothes on my back. I remember sitting on the steps of the empty house, crying out to God and having a conversation with Him, asking Him what I was going to do and why it had to be me. I was thinking what else could happen to me and what could be worse. I had nothing but the clothes on my back, and I was homeless.

Being Homeless

I thought about my mother in Alabama, but I didn't want to go back home in that condition—a cast on my wrist and nothing but the clothes on my back. I was too embarrassed to do that. Pride wouldn't allow me to make the call and have her send me money to come home.

My mother knew I wasn't happy, but she didn't know the extent of my unhappiness.

I had gotten a job at the Pentagon soon after moving to DC. After I got the job at the Pentagon, I called and told my mother where I was working. She told me how proud she was. With her telling me that, I began to change my mind about moving back home and staying—not in my marriage. I lost my job after that because I had missed so many days from work for the little time I had been there. I left the house, walking and still having a conversation with God.

It was getting dark, and I had no place to go. I walked to the same area where I had slept in my car, which was at a shopping center. I went in and out of stores until they all began to close. I looked around the parking area, and I saw two dumpsters beside each other in the parking lot. As I looked at the dumpsters, I contemplated getting into the space between them to spend the night and hide and possibly be safe. That thought immediately left my mind because of the smell from the dumpsters. I don't know how that thought even entered my head, now that I think about it. It's almost comical because I have OCD. There are various forms of OCD, and sleeping between a dumpster would have either cured the type that challenged me or taken me further into a mental place I wasn't willing to go.

I began walking back toward the empty house. I thought about breaking a window to get inside and spend the night there.

As I was walking around the house looking for a window that I could break and get through, I suddenly heard someone call my name and asked me if I was okay. It was my neighbor. She scared the fire out of me because I didn't see or hear her come up. After I recognized who she was, I erupted into tears and couldn't stop. I began crying and saying to her I have no place to go. She took me into her house, and I spent the night there. She sat and talked with me most of the night. I talked, and she listened. She said that when she saw the moving company van at my house, she thought it was strange because we had been in the house less than two months and she had not seen me for a week. She asked if I had any relatives in the area, and a light went on in my mind. I had forgotten about my cousin Deborah and Gerald whom I had called before and who took me to the hospital. When your mind is overloaded sometimes, you can't think and you forget important things. The next morning, I called my cousin Deborah. She came over and picked me up from my neighbor's house. I ended up staying with them for a couple of months.

Things we go through to reach our purpose are perplexing and mind-boggling. The steps we go through to get to God's plans are what make life worth living. There is a quote often heard in churches from pastors in the pulpits that says, "You go through to get to." The questions I have asked myself while going through what I have gone through were, Is it divine design, or did I go through life based upon decisions and choices I made on my own?

When you look back over your life, can you honestly say to yourself, concerning your circumstance and situation, that if it took all that you went through to get to where you are today, would you go through it again? The answer depends on where you are today in life. If where you are today is in a good place, you would answer yes. You would go through it again. If where you are is the opposite and your path is rough and rocky, you would answer no. You would not go through it again.

Take a minute and reflect upon where you are this very moment in your life. I hope you're in a good place, but if not, I can assure you that if you hold on to your faith and know that where you are is temporary and not only for the glory of God but for your glory as well, you will sustain yourself. When we stop and ask ourselves questions, it is a good thing because it makes us question our motives and actions. Are they good or bad? The choices or decision you are about to make—will they help you or hurt you? One of the most valuable lessons I learned but didn't learn soon enough is to ask questions of myself to myself. If I had done this sooner in life, I could have avoided so many things. This is where free will comes into play in your life. We all have been given free will. Now the question you should ask yourself is whether it is divine design, God's will, or your will.

From the cotton fields, leaving home after graduating high school, moving to Chicago to live with my sisters and not have anyone to answer to, getting my first job, and having my own money, I thought I had hit the million-dollar lottery. I felt like I had escaped slavery, entered freedom, and reached the promised land.

Life's directions have a way of throwing major curveballs at you. You're constantly at the bat, and balls are steadily being thrown at you. You keep swinging at the ball and striking out. You stay on the mound, swinging with the bat because you feel that at some point, eventually, you're going to hit it and make a home run. Finally, you get lucky and hit the ball, and you begin to run to first base, but before you can get your foot off the mat to begin running, the back catcher, pitcher, and first baseman are upon you, trying to put you out.

You begin to run faster back and forth so you won't be caught, but somewhere within that run, as you are trying to make it to first base, you get tired, let your guard down, and slip or fall, and the next thing you know, you hear it spoken loud and clear: You're out!

The game is fun as long as you're in control. You can come and go as you please, but after a while, the game begins wearing you out and you're caught in the middle of trying to reach first base. From that point on, it seems like you're constantly trying to reach first base before being caught and put out. Sometimes life's circumstance is just like a baseball game and you trying to get to the home plate.

After leaving the cotton field, every life experience appeared exciting, and it was. Even in the midst of heartaches, disappointment, and pain, when I look back, life is a continuous stream of excitement and trying to reach first base and being caught off guard. Life's struggles build character, and it's up to each individual if they label and name their struggles. I chose to and labeled myself and my character as strength—strength for my struggles.

The excitement of seeing the outcome is what gives you the motivation to continue moving. Life only stays the same when you have no hope and when you stop moving. When you know that your life is not your own but for the fulfillment of God's will, you won't mind the interruptions because you know there is a greater purpose ahead of what you're experiencing at the moment. Sometimes the pit or the interruptions take place to allow your purpose to catch up to where you are.

So often, we get ahead of our destiny on our own. Because of God's grace and mercy, He lets us grow on our own for a while. He allows us to venture off to what we think should be taking place and let us do our own thing until we realize we've messed up and learn to appreciate where we should be.

He allows this, so we will know that we can do nothing without Him, that our life is not our own, and that we are only here temporarily to fulfill His will on earth.

The amazing thing about fulfilling His will is demonstrating to those who know you the awesomeness of His power. Life is a testimony. Whether good, bad, or indifferent, we all have a testimony. Proverbs 16:4 says, "The Lord has made all things for Himself, even the wicked, for the days of evil." Have you ever known someone, and when you see them years later, you look at them in amazement because of how they look? They look like what they have been through. Their lifestyle caught up with them, and they look broken, old, wounded, and defeated. Life has taken them on the course of a good hobbyhorse ride or a bad roller-coaster malfunction. Life makes some look good or look like death walking on two legs. Have you known someone at one point who's prospering and doing very well, and when you see them again, they are at the lowest place in life, destitute, or strung out in some form or another or vice versa? The first thing that enters your mind is, What in the world happened to them? Life has a way of catching up with us.

Should our lives be an open book to the world, especially to those that know you? Matthew 5:16 says, "Let your light so shine before men that they may see your good works and glorify your Father which is in heaven." People see Christ through us in our openness and transparency. We have allowed society to put demands upon us and became more concerned about how we're perceived in the eye of man more than God. If we take off the mask and be real, we will find out that the majority of people in this world are wearing a mask—from the White House to the Roman Cathedral. We all have some stuff that we don't want revealed. We hide behind a mask of deceit, brokenness, confusion, depression, anger, etc., yet we wonder why so many people are sick and unhappy or why the suicide rate is escalating daily. Homes are broken, and our children are messed up in the head because no one wants to be real and to tell life's truths. We get so lost in deception that we lose who we are spiritually, physically, emotionally, and mentally. We get comfortable living undercover and not open and honest with being who we are. No matter what we go through, we have to remain focused and true to ourselves and realize who we are and whose we are. How can the world continue and be as it is if the trials of life's experience are not exposed or opened to honesty so that those going through similar experiences know that they, too, can overcome and see the goodness of God and know that He lives and is real? I believe that my tribulations were for His glory, as well as mine.

Mutt Dear always told me even as a child that if I fell into a pile of s——t, I would come out smelling like a rose. One day, as I was going through and felt that I was about to give up, I remember crying out to God. He took me to this particular passage of scripture and spoke to me, letting me know that I was going to be okay. He spoke so loud into my spirit and resonated into the very fiber of my being. The sound wasn't heard in my ears as it does when reading aloud or talking. I felt the voice of God upon my heart, reaching the essence of my inner spirit and touching my soul. This was His way of reassuring me that He had me at that point and that I had to trust and hold on to Him through His Word.

When God speaks, it's hard to explain, but He speaks verbally and nonverbally. Yet He speaks. As I was about to give up, I felt and heard the words "Faint not." That was all I heard, and then I began hearing it again and again—"Faint not." At first, it can be somewhat confusing. I felt it instantly as calmness and peace came upon me so swiftly. It was as if the beat of my heart took on a rhythm that stopped and restarted instantly at the same time in a beat of joyfulness. The sadness of my heart stopped, and a new rhythm of peace picked up and replaced where I was in my emotional moment. That's the only way I can describe this. Emotions are felt, and the mind made a sound—that is how I believe God answers and speaks to me in times of need. Literally with my heart stopping and restarting. What I heard sounded so soft and sweet, then I heard it again, and that time, I realized it was the voice and move of God. Automatically I stopped having my pity party, and from my lips came "I desire that you *faint not* at my tribulations for you, which is your glory" (Ephesians 3:13).

It came from my lips, but it was not my voice that I heard. I believe even now that it was the Spirit of God that came from my lips. What was spoken that resonated so profoundly were two things: one, my tribulations and, two, His glory. God was telling me that He was allowing what I was experiencing at the time and that I would get the glory and victory in the end. God said for Shirley's cause, He bow His knees to God the Father in Shirley's behalf. Jesus was interceding for me. That showed me how special I am to Him, and He comforted me when I needed comforting.

After being homeless, I looked forward to going to the next phase because I knew I was being strengthened in my struggle. I knew something good would come out of where I was. It always did, and what Mutt Dear spoke in my life follows me today. The thing we must realize when we go through things is that we have choices. I could have chosen to stay in that place and continue my pity party, or I could choose to believe and trust the words that were spoken to me from God. What was spoken made me see that where I was, was only temporary. I didn't know how or when, but I knew I wouldn't be in that place forever. There was always something deep inside that reassured me that I was going to be okay, but the mind has a way of playing tricks on you when you don't stay focused on the Word of God. That same thing is inside each of us. God is no respecter of persons, and when we keep our mind focused on Him, He promises to keep us in perfect peace.

Just as God had a ram in the bush when Abraham was about to sacrifice his son, Isaac, God has a ram in the bush for us as well. Someone is always there for you when you least expect it. I began attending Mt. Ennon Baptist Church with my cousin Barbara in Fort Washington, Maryland. I became a member of the church and joined the choir. I've always liked singing, and the ladies in the choir became very close to me. In most Baptist churches, all choirs wear uniforms. My cousin Barbara and some of the other ladies bought me a skirt and blouse so that I would be in uniform with the other choir members. Many of the ladies in the choir knew my story because I shared my testimony with them, and they blessed me monetarily and spiritually.

After developing a relationship with the ladies, there was one lady in particular that I connected with, whom I called Lozzie. She was tall in stature like myself. We bonded like no other. She is the one person whom I shared my all with. I stayed at her house on the weekend, crying on her shoulders, and she encouraged me when she was going through some challenges of her own. Watching her go through her challenge gave me strength. She had a tumor in her brain, and the day before her surgery, the pastor and some of the ladies from the church went to her house to pray and encourage her.

As we entered her house, the aroma of freshly baked bread met us at the door. Lozzie had baked some homemade bread and began serving us with a million-dollar smile, laughing and encouraging us. She knew we were concerned about her. Observing her and what she was about to go through the next morning made me realize that my challenge was mild in comparison to what she was about to experience because brain surgery is a delicate, major, and sensitive procedure. I had lost material things, but her life was at risk. That made me realize all the more how blessed I was. What I had and didn't have was no comparison to what she was about to go through.

After her surgery the next day, I called the hospital to check on her, preparing myself to hear her husband, George, answer the phone. To my surprise, Lozzie herself answered the phone, sounding like an angel.

Her voice was strong, and I said to her, "When are you going to have the surgery?"

She laughed and said, "I had it this morning."

I began rejoicing because she sounded happy as if she had not gone through anything. She said to me, "Shirley Jean, what God just brought me through He can bring you through what you're experiencing too."

And that gave me so much joy and hope.

Chapter Three
Capitol Hill

I went to DC in search of a job. I rode the subway train to the union station. As I walked out of the station, I looked across the street and saw rows of flags blowing back and forth from the wind. Many people were around. Again, peace came over me as I walked across the street toward the flags. Behind the flags and across the street was a park. I walked through the park, and a sense of excitement mixed with joy and peace overwhelmed me. It was as if I was being directed there by an inner strength that was not of my own. As I continued walking, I looked up and saw the US Capitol, and the excitement intensified. I had seen pictures of the Capitol on television, in books, and in person many times, but something was so surreal about seeing it this time. I wanted to burst into laughter because I was so overjoyed. I didn't understand what was taking place and why. As I walked through the park, I saw buildings that looked inviting and exciting. I stopped in the middle of the park and just looked up in the trees. As I looked up, it was as if the leaves on the trees whispered to me. And I said to myself, "This is where I want to work."

I was having a private conversation with God because I didn't want people to think I was like some of the people I had just seen walking outside the union station, who were talking to themselves and asking for money. I was having this conversation in my mind, but all at once, I heard myself speaking and saying aloud, "This is where I want to work." What I spoke I released into the atmosphere, and something happened. God knew what I needed and knew my heart's desire, but I wanted the devil to hear it. I was determined that the devil in hell and nothing else could stop me and take away what I felt when I saw the Capitol. I have always heard people say you had to know someone on the Hill to get a job there.

When those thoughts entered my mind, I spoke aloud and said, "God, I know you."

There was an overwhelming force of assurance that pierced the soul of my spirit and gave me confidence that something was about to happen, which would be unexplainable. I literally felt and heard the voice of God when I spoke this. I had heard God's voice before, but to feel His voice and hear Him again, I knew something phenomenal was about to take place—something that was beyond my or anyone else's control. God and I had that kind of relationship, so I knew when I got that feeling, nothing was impossible. Something supernatural was about to take place.

The body is the outer court of a person, and the soul is the holy place of God. My spirit reacted to the holy of holies. What I spoke wasn't spoken by me. It didn't sound like me. It came from me, but that was not my voice. And because of the awesomeness of what happened and how it happened, I associated it to the holy presence of God. What was spoken was spoken with so much power, authority, truth, and conviction it couldn't have been anyone but God Himself. I felt the holy presence of God literally move because of the enormity in which it was spoken. It was spoken in such a way that it felt like the leaves and the breeze of the trees themselves had spoken to me again like it did when I was being called into ministry.

There were so many people going in and out of the buildings, which were the Hart, Dirksen, and Russell Senate offices.

The energy and excitement radiating from the people passing by was invigorating.

I stopped and asked someone where to go to apply for employment on the Hill, and they said, "You're standing in front of it."

And they directed me to go up the steps and through the double doors I was standing in front of. To my left would be the placement office.

I said, "Okay, God, You've placed me where I need to be, so I know You will show me what to do next and whom to talk with."

Things were transpiring so quickly I didn't have time to think about my appearance. I wasn't expecting to be interviewed. I was wearing a pair of jeans and an orange fleece pullover and sneakers. Remember, my wardrobe was limited. As I walked into the placement office, a young lady walked up to me and asked if she could help me. I told her I was interested in seeing the job announcement that was opened for employment on the Hill. She directed me to a computer and gave me a temporary password to log in to the system. She asked me if I saw anything that I was interested in to complete the application online.

As I began looking, I was becoming discouraged because I didn't qualify for what I saw, it appeared. I was reading job titles that intimidated me. I wasn't reading the descriptions associated with the title, I felt that the position qualified the job title. There was one particular title that kept alerting my conscience to pay closer attention to. I kept seeing the title over and over, which was listed as "Telecommunication Technical Support Specialist Analyst." I didn't read the job description since I thought it was beyond my qualifications from the way it sounded in my head when I read the title.

Suddenly, I felt an overwhelming urge to read the description, and was I ever surprised. If I had not been obedient to what the Spirit was saying to me, I would have missed out on my blessing. The job title was "Telecommunication Technical Support Specialist Analyst." As I read the description of the job, it was nothing more than a telephone operator. I had to contain myself after reading the description. I almost went into a fit of laughter after reading it. One of the first jobs I had when I lived in the UK was a telephone operator.

It's amazing how your past can trigger something in your subconscious and causes you to have a flashback of past experiences. To this day, I don't know how or why the experience I had with the counselor that asked me what I wanted to do when I finished school when I was in middle school resurfaced. After reading the job description, that incident popped into my memory, and right away, I thought, *What did that have to do with right now?*

Later, and even now as I write this, I think back, was it the job titles that triggered and set off doubt in my mind to make me think I could not do what was before me? The seed that had been planted in my mind by the counselor had nested in my subconscious and was hidden there. At that very moment, that seed wanted to give birth to come alive and stop me from doing what I was destined to do. I allowed that seed to resurrect, and a simple description with an enticing long title intimidated and put doubt in me. I believe with everything in me that I could have been a gynecologist if I had pursued it.

After completing the online application, no sooner had I hit the send button the young lady who approached me when I walked in came to me and said they were interviewing for the position I had just applied for. She asked me if I had time for an interview. I was so excited I didn't think about what I was wearing, which were jean and sneakers. I immediately said yes.

The person who was to do the interviewing wasn't there in that office. She was across the hall in the telecommunication office. I was given a room number and sent across the hall, and someone would be waiting for me. The person waiting was the supervisor of the department. I will never forget her. Once I heard her name, I had that same overwhelming peace come upon me again as it did in the park. Her name was the same as mine; her name was Shirley.

When we met, I apologized to her for my appearance, and she told me that was okay. Instantly something clicked between the two of us. The chemistry was so affectionate. There was a connection that seemed familiar and personable, and I felt as if I had known her all my life. I liked her a lot. My interview with her lasted over an hour. After the interview and talking with her, she asked me when could I start working. I opened up and shared my story with her about the situation I was in. I told her that I didn't have any clothes and that what I was wearing was all I had. She told me she would put me on the night shift because her department was a twenty-four-seven day operation. By being on the night shift, no one would notice my clothes as long as they were clean. From the things we talked about, I knew God was still with me. She was an angel He was using to help me. Tears began welling in my eyes, and I couldn't hold them back. Tears began rolling down my face. She walked around her desk, and I remember her putting her arms around me. It felt like the weight of the world was lifted from me. Her arms around me were so comforting. I just knew they were the arms of God Himself. Shirley Blackburn was her name. Her arms around me were the avenue used for me to get on Capitol Hill. I will forever remember that, and I am eternally grateful. She has since gone to be with the Lord.

All that took place from the time I stepped out of the union station. What happened afterward, especially on the Hill, was unprecedented. Because I had previously worked internationally, I had a security clearance that gave credence in being hired without waiting for a background security check. I began working the following week on the night shift. That was the door that opened for me and got me on Capitol Hill. That began my journey of twenty-two years on the Hill. I worked in telecommunications for two years and, later, began working for the SSAA (Senate Sergeant at Arms) accounting office. Twenty-two years later, I retired as a financial administrative office manager at the office of Senator John D. Rockefeller IV.

There are one hundred senators in office on the Hill. Of those one hundred senators, there are one hundred administrative managers. Out of the one hundred managers, there were only five of color who held that position, and I was one of the five. I was accountable for maintaining a budget of 2.3 million dollars a year. At the end of the fiscal year, I was accountable for every penny spent and wasn't allowed to exceed one cent over that budget. I would have lost my job if I did not maintain that budget. Math was one of the worst subjects in school for me, but with Mutt Dear and Big Mama's teachings, I mastered that budget to the very penny with common sense. I held that position without completing a college degree.

Working on the Hill was interesting, exciting, and challenging. My cotton field and Alabama experiences prepared, equipped, and qualified me for what I experienced on the Hill. I graduated from Alabama's cotton fields with an associate, master's, bachelor's, doctorate, triple doctorate, and every possible degree life and the world had to offer. I've mentioned many times throughout my journey that nothing we go through in life is without purpose. How we embrace each experience qualifies us for the next phrase. Twenty-two years on the Hill was no picnic. I experienced challenges, you name it. It's there, just different scenarios. Racism, prejudice, hatred, backbiting, jealously, envy, and all the ugliness of life follow and find you no matter where you go. I was on the Hill six months when I experienced the boldest, most blatant, and most overt form of prejudice and racism I had ever experienced.

Applying For A Loan

Six months after I began working on the Hill, I applied for a personal loan at the Senate credit union. The loan officer who took my application was to notify me within a few hours if the loan was approved or not. I didn't hear back from him that day. The credit union was next door to the office where I worked. Literally I could walk out of the back door of my office and walk directly into the credit union. The next day, I walked over to inquire on the loan. As I entered the credit union, I asked to speak to the loan officer who took my loan application. He was available, and I was directed to his office. As soon as I entered his office, he came at me so abruptly before I could open my mouth. It startled me. He was so rude that I had to ask him if I had done something wrong. He told me that my application wasn't approved. The tone he used was so demeaning and unprofessional that I almost cried. I tried asking him some questions, but he cut me off before I could complete the question. I wanted to know if the loan was denied because of my credit score or if it was because I hadn't been employed long enough in the Senate.

One of the things Mutt Dear taught us as children was to establish credit, and once you do, always pay your bills on time. She taught us that we would not always have money to pay for what we wanted or needed in life. She told us that good credit is as good as having cash. I can't begin to tell you how much she stressed that to me and my siblings. Even in the midst of me being in the situation I was in, I had contacted the creditors I owed during my divorce when I was left with nothing. I made arrangements with them so that I would not be turned over to the collections agency. Because the loan I had applied for wasn't approved, I wanted to be sure that wasn't the reason for the denial. The reason he gave me had nothing to do with my credit score, but his own personal, racist, bigoted views.

He personally took it upon himself not to approve my loan. He never submitted the application. He stated, "You people, you always want to buy things you can't afford and borrow money you don't pay back. If you people stop buying cars and expensive clothes, you would have some money."

I applied for a personal loan of a thousand dollars, and he said to me, "You don't have a thousand dollars that you have to take out a loan for it. You're pitiful."

He told me to come back in a year, and by then, if I needed a thousand dollars, he might consider letting me have it. I was so appalled I couldn't speak. I didn't say a word, I walked out of the credit union, went back to my office, got back on the telephone board, and began working. I was in shock. I sat at my desk and had to think if what just took place really happened. Did that person just say all those things to me? Was I having a flashback of experiences when I lived in Alabama? did I imagine what had happened? Had my mind played tricks on me? As I thought about how I was talked to and the tone in which I was talked to sounded, I tried to hold back tears but couldn't. As tears began running down my face, I got up from my desk and walked toward the break room. My intention was to go to the ladies room so that no one would see me crying. I was headed that way when I left my desk. Before I reached the break room, anger had taken over. I was headed back to the credit union.

To exit the office from the location of the break room this time, I exited the front of the office where the receptionist desk was. Sandra, the receptionist at the front desk, noticed I was upset and saw that I was crying. I didn't realize she had followed me. She caught up with me and asked me if I was okay. I was so upset I could barely talk. She gave me a minute to compose myself and kept telling me to just calm down or else I was going to be sick. After I calmed down, I told her what happened. I became more upset just repeating it. There was a police station outside the office, and the officer on duty also noticed me crying. He and Sandra talked with me until I calmed down.

From everything that I had gone through in Alabama—experiencing prejudice and racism and literally being slapped so hard by a white man that I can recall every detail and see the flashes of light that appeared as stars—and on top of everything else I had been through, I had reached my cap. My volcano was at the peak of explosion. At that moment, I didn't know how much or what else I could take. What the loan officer said was more painful than being slapped. In addition to what I was experiencing personally, I had reached a limit of overload. I think I was operating under adrenaline up until that point. As the saying goes, "The straw broke the camel's back," that was the straw that had pushed me to my limit. Being talked to like that while I was in desperate need of financial help, I believe I was capable of doing something to the loan officer barehanded. He didn't have a gun unlike the man at the auto dealership back in Alabama. I was going to the loan officer to snatch him out from behind his desk.

When I hear of people snapping in a workplace, I can somewhat identify. You never know what a person is going through or have gone through and having someone talk to you and treat you in a certain way in a time when you feel as if the bottom of your life has fallen out of your very existence and you're doing everything within your power to hold on to your last bit of sanity. Then you have someone come at you like this man did. It can cause you to go into a place in your mind that's not safe for you or the person that pushed you the wrong way. I was nearly there, and if it had not been for Sandra and Officer Rogers who came to my rescue and talked me back to sanity, who knows what would have happened? I had been in that place more than once in my life, and everything has a limit and a point. And that moment could have been that limit.

Sandra and Officer Rogers advised me to write a letter and go to the board members of the credit union and tell them what happened. In doing so, I discovered that there were several complaints similar to mine and that this person was already on probation. I received a phone call from a member of the board the next day, apologizing for what had taken place, and they informed me that the person had been terminated. My application was given to someone else, and the loan was approved. Again, God had put the right people in the right place at the right time to help me. He knew I had reached a limit, and He sent His angel again to direct me. Sandra and I became very good friends after that day. I gave her a name of endearment that day, and to this day, she is my Lucy. I often thank her because my Lucy saved my life, sanity, and my job that day.

Everyone needs a friend. A true friend will stand with you through thick and thin, and Lucy is a true friend. In everything I experienced on the Hill, Lucy was there for me. After thirteen years of being on the Hill, I was terminated and lost my job. I worked in the department of the sergeant at arms, which I loved, until my supervisor retired. After he retired, he was replaced by a female. That's when things changed and the nightmare began. She had a dislike for me, and I couldn't figure out why. In my yearly evaluation, which came from her, I received the worst evaluation I had ever received since being on the Hill. I was off work a lot because I was suffering from an illness that could not be diagnosed. I spent a lot of time going back and forth to different doctors.

One day, as I was feeling very ill, I walked out of the office to get some fresh air. Before I could make it outside, I passed out and was taken to the hospital. That time, I was taken to Georgetown University Hospital in DC, and it was there that a diagnosis was made by a specialist. I was off work for two weeks.

After two weeks off work, I was happy to go back. As I went into the office, I was super happy and excited to see my coworkers. I was laughing and teasing with them, but I noticed my excitement wasn't reciprocated. I went to my desk to log in to my computer and wasn't able to log in. The supervisor came to me and said she wanted to see me along with the director of the department in the conference room. There, I was told I was terminated and was no longer needed. I didn't ask why I was being terminated. I assumed it was because I had been out of work because of my illness. To say I was shocked is an understatement. I looked at them, and the only thing that came out of my mouth was "Whatever I have done, I am sorry." Then I was told that my job performance wasn't satisfactory. I was told to clear out my desk and was given a box to put my belongings in and that I would be escorted from the building by the Capitol police.

I went back to my workstation to clean out my desk. Dennis, one of my coworkers, came to me and said he was sorry. Outside the door of the office, two police officers were there to escort me out of the building after I clean out my desk. I stated that it wasn't necessary to be escorted out of the building. It was hard enough to have lost my job. To be escorted out was even more embarrassing. I was told that it was standard procedure to be escorted out because it was a federal building. As I was escorted out by the police, the assistant director of the department was with the police. As I reached my car, I turned to her. Tears were running down her face, and she embraced me and told me she was so sorry this had happened to me. She and I had always gotten along well. I left the building and went home. I called Lucy and told her what had happened before. I called my husband.

Some things that happen can be a blessing in disguise. Proverbs 3:5 says, "Trust in the Lord with all your heart, and lean not unto your own understanding."

Although my sickness had been diagnosed, it took a while for me to get back to normal. The time I was off work, God was allowing my body to heal. Exactly thirty days from the day I was terminated, I was lying in bed, talking to God. I told God I was ready to go back to work. No sooner than those words were released from my lips, the phone rang. It was the COS (Chief Of Staff) from Senator Harry Reid's office, calling to ask me if I was still interested in a position I had applied for in his office. The amazing thing about that call was that I didn't remember applying for a position to that office. David, the COS, asked if I could come in the next day for an interview. I went for the interview and got the job. I was back on the Hill.

I had to go back to the office of the person who terminated me to be reinstated for a Senate ID and parking permit. When I walked into the office, she was the first person I saw. When she looked up and saw me, she dropped her head. When God does something, He does it well. When I got back to Capitol Hill for my new position, my salary doubled, my position upgraded, and my salary surpassed those whom I knew were instrumental in my termination.

I had to go back occasionally to the same office I was terminated from for official business. There, I would see the supervisor who terminated me. On one occasion, I went there to transact some business. She had to do the transaction for me because no one else was there but her. This time, she had to look and talk to me directly. Eye contact was made. What I saw when she looked up at me was shame and guilt.

After completing the business, she said to me, "Shirley, can I say something to you?"

I looked at her directly in her eyes and said, "Sure, you can."

She said, "I want to apologize to you for what I did to you."

I asked, "What did you do to me?"

With my response, she hesitated and her color changed. She became flushed in the face and lowered her head. She proceeded to try to dress up a cute explanation as to what happened and why. She said she had to fire me and only did what she was told to do.

I said to her, "You were my supervisor, and I couldn't have been terminated by the director if he hadn't been given reasons by you to do so."

When I saw that our conversation was about to go in a direction that wasn't good, I accepted her apology and said to her that it was only a thirty-day vacation and that it was a blessing in disguise because God had better plans for me and I was in a better place than I was before she had terminated me. I did ask her what had I done to her. She stated that I had not done anything and that it wasn't me. She shared with me that she was in the process of getting a divorce. I couldn't get angry with her because when you go through a divorce, you have so many emotions and you go through so much. A lot of what a person in that situation says and does is not intentional. They react out of pain and anger. Because of what I had been through, I identified with her somewhat. If I had not been in a good place mentally and financially at that time, could I have responded differently? I don't know. You never know what you will or will not do until you're put in a position to act. It's only afterward that you can answer yes, no, maybe, or maybe not. Not all questions have answers until they're a fact. You answer to what you do, not what you think you would have done or will do.

Something entered my thoughts as our conversation ended. Whether it was true or not, her personal life had been circulating throughout the office. If this was true, I could have filed a grievance concerning my termination. It wasn't worth the efforts or energy to go in that direction because I was in a good place. She was in a biracial marriage. Her husband, a man of color, had left her and was dating a woman of color. And because I was a woman of color and the only female in the office, she was directing her anger toward me. Race never leaves your mind when you've experienced so much of it all your life. I don't want to see or look for a black-and-white motive behind every situation, but in my experiences in life, it's never far behind.

Senator Harry Reid

Thirty days after my termination, I was back on the Hill as the front administrative manager for Senator Harry Reid, who was majority leader at the time. You never know what impression you make upon people by just being kind and smiling. David, the COS for Senator Reid, said to me doing my interview that I was one of the first people he thought of when the position came open in his office. He said he thought of me because the position I was being interviewed for I had one of the most important qualifications for the position. Being a people person with a sociable and pleasant personality. He said he had seen those qualities in me in the office I was terminated from. It was my interaction, friendliness, smile and how I made people feel comfortable under stressful situations that he admired about me. The office where I had previously worked was chaotic and could be stressful if you allowed it to be. It takes a person with special skills to work under stressful situations, especially when dealing with people with mutable personalities.

Things were going very well. My joy had returned, and I had recovered from my illness. There was so much joy and peace in my new environment in Senator Reid's office. But such as life, all good things come to an end. September 11, 2001, my good thing and America's good thing came to an end. There was a terrorist attack against the United States.

As I would arrive each morning for work, the first thing I would do when I entered the office is turn on the television in the receptionist area. Majority of the front offices in the Senate have televisions, and all of them are tuned in to CNN. The only time I ever saw a television not on CNN was when there was a Senate hearing that is not televised by major networks. I turned on the television but wasn't paying any attention to what was going on. As I was doing my morning routine, turning on the television, lights, and my computer I was about to change from my sneakers into my heels, which I kept underneath my desk. I wore sneakers to work daily. I had a forty-five-minute commute to and from work, and I would put my sneakers on after getting dressed from home to make the forty-five-minute drive into work. After arriving to work and parking my car in the parking deck of the Thurgood Marshall Building, I would walk a half block to my office, in the Dirksen Building. Wearing sneakers made my walk more comfortable; along with the drive.

As I was about to change into my heels, there was a newsbreak that came on the television, stating that an airplane had flown into one of the twin towers of the World Trade Center in New York City.

Other staff members were coming into the office for work, so I said to them, "Have you all heard what happened?"

And all eyes were staring at the television. The room was so quiet you could hear—as my grandmother would say—a mouse p——— on cotton. When the next announcement was made that the second tower was hit by another plane, we all began to panic. The entire office went into panic mode. I remember David, the chief of staff, coming out of his office with a look on his face that I think we all had at that moment. When David said that

Senator Reid was over at the Capitol in his official leadership office and they were evacuating him and other senators into the safe place that was designated for senators if there was a threat to the government, I knew it was time to get out the building.

Another news break came over the television stating that the Pentagon had been attacked. An airplane had crashed into its side, and by then, the evacuation alarms in the Senate buildings were going off for everyone to evacuate the building immediately. I was so thankful that I still had my sneakers on. When the alarms went off, the elevators were automatically shut off. I grabbed my purse and began walking down the five flights of stairs in a panic, like the hundreds of other people.

I was back at the parking deck of the Thurgood Marshall Building when I turned and looked around behind me. I looked back because I heard people running and I heard cries, screaming, and sirens coming from all over the area. When I looked back, I thought about a biblical story, where Lot told his wife not to look back when they were leaving the city of Sodom and Gomorrah. He told her if she looked back, she would turn into a pillar of salt. I did look back, and what I saw was devastating. It reminded me of what the Bible's description of what the world will look like when it comes to an end. People will be running, and there will be crying with no place to go. Many of the people who left their office had left without getting their purse or personal belongings. If they were able to reach their car, they wouldn't have keys to drive, or if they got home, they wouldn't have keys to get into their homes. According to the news and many people that I knew and talked with, it took some of them eight to fourteen hours to get home. I got to my car, and I was out of the parking deck and on my way home and don't remember getting home. I was crying and praying the entire time. My drive home was a forty-five-minute drive on a busy day, but it didn't take me any time—so it seemed that day—to get home.

I know I made it home within an hour. It was as if I was lifted out of the chaos in DC by the Spirit of God and put into my house in a matter of minutes in Waldorf, Maryland.

As I sat on my bed with my television on, watching the news from my bedroom, I tried calling Larry, my husband, but couldn't reach him. He worked as a driver at the White House for the vice president's office. There was no cell phone service anywhere in the city, and I couldn't reach him. As I watched the news and saw the devastation in New York, the Pentagon, and in Pennsylvania, I fell on my knees and began praying and weeping like the world had come to an end. I was so worried about my husband. I was home for several hours before I heard from him.

I was still sitting on my bed when I heard the front door to our house open. I exited the bedroom and went to the top of the steps, and there stood Larry, looking up at me like he had been through hell, with tears running down his face. We didn't speak a word. We looked at each other, met each other halfway in the middle of the stairs, and held on to each other as we cried together. Our tears were tears of appreciation and thanks that we both were safe. And our tears were for others from the panic we saw and the cries, pain, and fear we heard coming from others running through the streets of DC and what we knew had happened in our country.

After holding each other for what seemed like forever, we were finally able to speak. We expressed our fear of what had happened and could have happened to us. The first thing Larry said to me was he was trying to find me and he couldn't get on the hill. He was scared because he didn't know where I was. The feeling was mutual. My fear was that if a plane could get that close to the Pentagon and cause that much destruction, it could reach the White House as well, and I knew that's where my husband was.

Larry, my third and final marriage of twenty years, was truly a marriage of love, but alcohol consumed his life. He died in 2016.

The scenes of that day—of 9/11—will forever be in my memories. Each year since that day, I find myself revisiting some of the memories as the anniversary of that day nears. It has gotten better, but like my cotton-field experiences, certain memories never go completely away.

Senator Rockefeller

After working for Senator Harry Reid of Nevada, I was offered a job to work for Senator John D. Rockefeller of West Virginia.

The amazing thing about transitioning from one senator's office to another is the respect the senators have for one another when it came to staff leaving one office for another. Before transitioning, there had to be mutual agreement between the two senators. They don't take each other's employees without approval and consent being in agreement. This is in respect to the senator so that there will be no conflict between the two. I admired the policy that those two senators had with one another. I cannot speak for other offices if this was their policy as well, but I know this to be true between Reid and Rockefeller.

I loved working for both senators, and I liked the staff. I was with Senator Reid's office for less than a year. I wasn't looking for a new position when I left his office. It found me. After I was terminated from the sergeant at arms office, Senator Reid's office hired me and got me back on the Hill. I was so thankful to David, the COS, for Senator Reid that I didn't want to leave so soon. It was a better opportunity and position offered to me, and I would be able to use more of my financial skills.

Rockefeller's administrative manager, Aleysha, was leaving to work in the private industry. She told me about the vacancy coming up in that office and asked if I would be interested and would like to apply for the position. I didn't know Aleysha that well. I saw her in passing because our offices were two doors from each other. She knew I had previously worked for accounting at the Senate sergeant at arms office and had the experience needed for that position. I applied and was interviewed four times by different staff in Rockefeller's office. The last interview I had was with Senator Rockefeller, and I liked him immediately. We had something in common. We both were tall. He said it felt good to be able to talk with someone that he could look eye to eye with. He stood 6'7", and I am 6'1". He indicated that he would love to have me join his staff, but he had to talk with Senator Reid to get his approval before he would say yes to me becoming part of his staff. He didn't want to take someone from another senator's staff if it would cause problems, and I respected that.

Two weeks later, I began working for Senator Rockefeller. I was on the Rockefeller staff about a week before anthrax was discovered in Senator Daschle's office. The entire Hart and Dirksen buildings were evacuated and had to be shut down. I had not settled in and was still in the process of learning their names and learning my way around the office. With all that was going on, we did not skip a beat. Work continued. After evacuating and the building was shut down to be inspected by the Center for Disease Control and Environmental Protection Agency, we all were sent home. We weren't sure if we would be going to work the next day because we didn't know where to go or had a place to go. The Senate sergeant at arms office was working to find places to relocate those that had been misplaced by the anthrax. We did know that we would be out of the building for quite some time.

I received a called at home late that night from Ellen, the Legislative Director for Senator Rockefeller, telling me that we would meet the next day at her house in Arlington, Virginia. This was a surprise to me, and I thought of how dedicated this office was that someone would have an entire staff into their home to work. I was the new kid on the block, and my work involved personnel and finance issues therefore, I didn't think I was needed because they were legislative and would be discussing legislative issues.

After arriving the next morning at the LD's home, I discovered that it was twofold the reason being there. We all needed that connection because we had been through so much emotionally and mentally with 9/11, and now we were facing another traumatic experience: we had to stay connected to each other. Although the staff was new and different from my previous coworkers with Reid's office, I needed that connection. We all did.

Being in a close environment at the LD's house was a good thing. When people go through traumatic experiences together, personal contact is the best medicine. I didn't know the staff that well, and that was my opportunity of getting to know them. Ellen's house was large, but with that many people in one place, it appeared small. That closeness worked in our favor. We all became close, being in the small space. We were notified the next day that we would be transitioning to the Russell Building into one of the committee hearing rooms. That area was small as well, and that continued the unity, bonding, love, and connection we had for one another.

When the day came that we were able to move back into our office in the Hart Building, the timing was perfect. We had spent enough time with each other in such close quarters, so we all were ready for the solitude of our own space. Nearly three months of working that closely together has limits. We were out of the Hart Building from October 15, 2001, through January 22, 2002.

As the administrative manager, I was fortunate enough to have my own private office. That was a rarity and blessing in more ways than one for me and for the staff. There are not many private offices in a senator's office. The majority of the offices were set up with modular furniture that was separated and divided with a partition that didn't give much privacy. Not only did I do the financial and personnel duties of the office, I also became the office go-to person for counseling and personal matters. Whenever someone had a personal or private issue, they came to my office and closed the door. I would know then that it was time for personal and private talking. They shared many of their private struggles and frustrations with me. Of course, this wasn't part of my job, but I didn't mind at all. I felt honored that they thought enough of me and felt comfortable coming to me. They felt they could talk with me and knew I didn't take it lightly. It could have been that they came to me too because I was in seminary school at the time, studying to get my licenses in ministry, so they sensed a presence of comfort that made them comfortable. I am not sure if anyone knew at the time that I was in school to be licensed for ministry. They just knew that they had someone to talk to, and I was there for them. They trusted me and knew that whatever was said behind those doors would never leave those doors.

Jim, the COS, left the office as the chief of staff about three years after I came in. I loved working with Jim, and after he left, things began to change. There was a continuous turnover, and the new staff members were from a different era and were much younger. When I came on the staff, there were others who were my age, and I noticed that they began to leave as well. That left me being the oldest person in the office other than the senator. A better use of the term that I prefer to describe people of age is a "mature person."

I have seen this happen many times in workplaces. I tell people to this day, "Keep living. Your day will come to be the only mature person in your position, and when it happens, then your turn will come and you will experience the pain and disappointment that come with it as you are forced to leave because of age. It's done diplomatically, but it doesn't take a rocket scientist to realize what is happening."

As people reach a certain age, the system changes and does things to deter and try to persuade the mature into early retirement or resignation. In my lifetime, I've watched this tactic used in many industries of the workforce—whether private, civilian, or government. The eye-opener in this is that no matter who you are, if you've been a participant of this tactic or just a bystander, your day will come. What goes around comes around, or in simpler terms, karma will come back to visit you.

Rockefeller's leadership position caused changes in his personal office, which affected staff and payroll. This caused cutbacks in staff and payroll, which meant some would be losing their jobs and others would transition into the new leadership office. Working for a senator had its risks, come reelection time. If a senator was up for reelection and didn't win the election, that meant those working for that senator lost their job as well, unless they were picked up by the incumbent senator. I had the unfortunate task of telling some of the staff that their service was no longer required after Rockefeller's assignment changed and that they would be losing their job. That was one of the hardest things in the world to tell someone. The first thing they would say when I told them was "What am I going to do?" That was so heartbreaking. Some of them would shed tears, which made it all the harder for me. I wasn't sure if it was a question or a statement because they didn't know what else to say. After doing that and going through the emotional heartbreak with them, I didn't realize it but I was next in line. I was terminated, but my termination had a different twist behind it.

When you pray for something, be willing to accept the answer, however it comes. I had been contemplating retirement and moving back home to Alabama. I wanted to move back to Alabama to be close to family but was uncertain of what to do, when to do it, and how to do it. I got my answer when I lost my job with Rockefeller.

In my transition, what was meant for evil turned into good. Dog-eat-dog competing, backbiting, and all types of treachery appear when one fears that their meat will be taken off the bone and when all that would be left is the bone. Things become competitive and would resort to evil when it comes to livelihood. Because Rockefeller was downsizing his personal office, seven years of my satisfactory performance all at once became questionable and unsatisfactory. My maturity was no longer necessary or needed, and whatever I did from then on became unsatisfactory to Kerry, the COS. That was a way of decreasing staff and distributing work and salary to the less mature. What I was doing as one person would be distributed among three others, and my salary would be shared three ways to the less matured staff.

The love for money manifests its truth as the Bible speaks in 1 Timothy 6:10: "The love of money is the root of all evil." Selfishness is the seed that breeds evil. Self-interest makes people think more of themselves than others when it comes to money. Money is good to have. Everyone wants and needs it, but never let the love of it be the thing that soils your soul. It soils the soul when it becomes so important to you that you're willing to assassinate a person's character and destroy relationships and friendships for your self-interest. Rockefeller's new assignment had a lot of the staff afraid that they would be losing their jobs, and many began using devious tactics to make sure they would not be among those who would lose their position.

Alabama's cotton fields had once again strengthened me for the setup and disappointment to take me through another life struggle. Philippians 4:11–13 describes it better than I ever could. It says, "I am not saying this because I am in need, for I have learned to be content whatever the circumstances. I know what it is to be in need, and I know what it is to have plenty. I have learned the secret of being content in any and every situation, whether well fed or hungry, whether living in plenty or in want. I can do all this through Christ who gives me strength" (KJV).

I was disappointed and upset when I was told I had to leave, but I was in a better position to leave more so than the others who had gone before me. I had the age and the years to retire. After I was given the notification to leave, I was told I would remain on payroll for three months. Things began to fall into place, and I was blessed beyond my wildest imagination and expectation.

I went into the office three days after my notice and began clearing out my desk and removing personal things, getting things in place for the person who would replace me. There were three persons of color in the office at that time. When I was told I was terminated, I called them in their homes that night after work to tell them I would be leaving and to tell them what had happened. One of them was very sympathetic and even shed tears with me, while the other one's response was so shocking I was taken aback. When I shared with her what had happened, there was not a word of encouragement or heartfelt compassion. She began telling me that she would apply for my position and hoped she could move into my office and hoped it wouldn't be given to someone else. For a second, I thought I was hearing the wrong thing and wondered if she understood what I had just said to her. Her excitement of getting part of my salary and the private office was not mistaken because she proceeded to tell me her plans of her retirement and what her salary would be if she was given my position.

I thought, *How selfish and insensitive.* And I immediately got off the phone with her. I was hurt and broken more by what she said and did not say after being told I was no longer needed and was losing my job.

After a few days of mentally processing what had taken place, I had such a peace, and with that peace, I knew that I was going in the right direction. God had shown me this scripture one night as I was praying about what to do, and in that hour of prayer, the Holy Spirit took me to the book of Psalms in the bible. Psalm 32: 8 said, "I will instruct you and teach you in the way you should go, and I will guide you with my eye." I knew and felt instantly that God had stepped down from heaven and spoke directly to me. I felt more peaceful and was happier at that very moment, and I knew I was going to be okay. I didn't miss a blessed step in the transition.

I called my son in Alabama and asked him to find me a Realtor, and I would fly down the following week and begin looking for a place to live. The housing industry at this time was at its lowest for buying homes. Selling was a different story. The economy was headed in the direction of a recession, and homes were hard to sell. I had a house in Charles County, Maryland, and the mortgage on it was no chump change. I put my house on the market anyway, in spite of the economy. I had three months to make some fast moves to stay ahead of the game. I would remain on payroll three months with the Senate, and when I found a house and a credit report was done, it would show I was employed and had an income. As long as it was done within those three months, no one had to know the details. I wasn't worried about my credit. I knew it was good. I didn't know what would happen after that, but I also knew I would not be able to maintain two mortgages.

Things were continuing in my favor in spite of what I was thinking, seeing, or feeling. God and I had a long conversation, and I didn't have to tell Him my fears. He was aware of them, and He was resolving the situations minute by minute. When you get out of the way and step back to trust God, He does the unspeakable. He dots every *i* and crosses every *t*. He makes the worst situation perfect, and who else makes perfect perfect but the one who is perfect? In every situation we go through, we have to trust that the process is not always as it appears to the natural eye, the natural mind, or the natural man.

I didn't have to worry about my existing mortgage. God had orchestrated that there was a ram in the bush. Shirley, a friend whom I had met in Europe and known for a while, got an assignment to relocate into the Virginia and DC area. She needed a place to live. I told her I was moving back to Alabama and that she could stay at my house until the house was sold. She agreed to that and offered to make the mortgage payment on the house as rent for staying there until she could find a place of her own. That was perfect. Another *i* was dotted in the process in my favor.

I flew home that weekend, but the night before I was to fly out, God and I were having our continuous conversation about my direction. I saw a vision of a house in my prayer conversation while I was talking with God. I saw a house with three lights hanging from the ceiling at the kitchen counter, and I saw an open family room that connected to the kitchen, where the light was hanging. That's all I saw. I went to bed that night and had a dream and saw the same in my dream.

I awakened the next morning to finish packing. As I was about to pack my laptop, there was an overwhelming urge that came upon me to open up the laptop and look at something.

I was obedient to what I was being directed to do with the laptop and had no clue what to look for. I had been on my laptop last night, looking at houses in the areas I wanted to look at while in Alabama. As I logged in to a website, from out of nowhere popped up houses that I had not seen before, and the first house that caught my eye was a house with pictures of the exact images I had dreamed and seen in my vision. The address was written in bold letters. I couldn't help but see it. I wrote down the address to bring with me, after that, I logged out and closed the laptop, I didn't look at anything else. I didn't feel the need to. I knew I had seen what I was supposed to see.

I flew into the Huntsville Airport in Alabama. I only had two days to do what I needed to do in Alabama, and I didn't have time to waste. The Realtor, Tisha, my son's friend, met me, and that entire day had been set aside to look at houses. I told her I had an address of a house I wanted to see. She told me that she had a few houses she wanted to show me, and after I looked at what she had, she would take me to the address I had written down. The houses she wanted to show me were in Muscle Shoals, which was about an hour's drive from the airport in Huntsville. The address I had was also in Muscle Shoals.

I wasn't paying any attention to where she was taking me. I was just looking out at houses in the development from the window of her car, and she never said aloud the address she was taking me. I still had not paid any attention to the address of the first house she showed me as we pulled up into the driveway. I liked the neighborhood, but all I was interested in was the address I had. As I walked into the house, it was like I had been there before and I belonged there. The family area was the first thing I saw when I walked into the house. It was open and spacious. I liked it.

When I saw the kitchen and the three lights hanging over the kitchen countertop, I said to her, "This is the house I saw in my vision."

I asked her the address, and it was the same as I had written. We did a walk-through, and I liked everything about the house. This was it. I told her to begin the paperwork for a contract. She insisted that I should take a look at one more of the houses before I made a final decision. I went along with her, but my mind was already made up. I am sure she was doing her job before she put down the contract. I know it was unheard of to buy the first house you see, and she may have felt a responsibility to assure I was making the right decision.

After showing me the second house, she realized that nothing could change my mind. I asked her to take me back to the first house, and I did another walkthrough. I wanted to go back because I wanted to have another conversation with God about the house. The house had been on the market for a while. The owner had taken a job out of state, and he was somewhat in the predicament I was in. He was paying two mortgages and wanted to eliminate one of the mortgage payments. I had my Realtor call the owner and ask if he would go down on the cost. While she was getting in contact with him and the agency that was marketing the house, God and I were having another conversation. I said to God, "I know this is the house You showed me and wanted me to have, but will you lower the cost for me?"

I was standing in the middle of the family room, having my private conversation with God, while Tisha was on the phone, talking with the owner and his Realtor. She came to me and said he refused to lower the cost. I was disappointed at that news and walked outside and around the house, still admiring it and continuing my conversation with God.

As she was locking up, I stood in the front yard, and I said to God once again, "God, I want this house."

Tisha had finished locking up the house. We got back into her car. As we were backing out of the driveway, her cell phone rang, and it was the owner's Realtor. They had agreed to lower the cost and sell to me at the cost I asked for. All I could do was say "thank you" God, and I shared my testimony with Tisha, and she began rejoicing with me.

Two days later, I was back on the plane headed back to Maryland, and things in Alabama were in process. I stayed in constant contact with Tisha. A credit report was done. The loan for the house was approved.

Three weeks later, I flew back to Alabama, signed all the necessary papers, and was given a key to my new address in Alabama. To move that expeditiously was unheard of when buying a new home. When God is working, nothing is impossible. Psalm 147:15 says, "He sent out His command to the earth. His word ran very swiftly." When God puts things in place, there is no limit to what can and cannot happen. He had put a command on that particular house for me, and the process was swift.

Meeting Senator Obama

Working on the Hill had its challenges. I experienced some wonderful things and had the opportunity to meet many wonderful, powerful, and prestigious people. Some of the people I was fortunate enough to have met and who left an impression and impacted our country in some way are Coretta Scott King, Condoleezza Rice, President Billy Clinton and Mrs. Clinton, President George W. Bush and Mrs. Bush, Vice President Al Gore and Mrs. Gore, President Dick and Mrs. Chaney, Dr. Ben Carson, Djimon Hounsou, Cicely Tyson, Danny Glover, and Isaiah Washington, to name a few.

I have been invited to sit at the table and dine with the ambassador of China at the Chinese Embassy in DC. I was privileged and honored to have been one of the first chosen to sit under the auspices of Dr. Barry Black, the first and only African American Chaplin to serve in the US Senate. Chaplin Black offered a ten-session biblical mentoring study program to

Senate employees, and I was one of the first to receive a certificate of completion through his teaching.

I have attended a Senate hearing where laws are put into place to govern our country. I've witnessed firsthand the real truth of what goes on behind closed doors in our government. It was surprising who actually put many laws into place that we live by. I was under the impression that the laws that are introduced and put into place were done by senators themselves because you see them on the flooring during the Senate hearing, defending what they wanted passed and put into law. I learned that much of what is brought before the Senate is brought by young freshmen coming out of college. They come to the Hill fresh out of college as legislative aides, with ideas and suggestions and then present them to the Senate and the senators, and the next thing you know, it's on the Senate floor, being argued and debated by the senator to be voted and put into law.

It made sense after I realized that young people are the future. They see a change that needs to take place, and the only way those changes could happen was for them to get in the ear of the senator and bring to them new ideas of things that should be revised and implemented. This is a new era, and the world cannot continue to operate under laws that were put in place hundreds of years ago. Majority of the senators that are in Congress have overstayed their term and should retire. The young people know that's not going to happen; therefore, they use to their advantage how to get things done, and that is to get in the ear of the senator and persuade them to speak in their behalf. What we see on the media is only a tip of the iceberg of what actually takes place behind closed doors in our government.

I spent many days walking the halls of Capitol Hill, praying and interceding, asking God to send people and leaders with a heart like His. There were so many interesting things I experienced on the Hill, but the most memorable of them all was meeting Barack Obama. I met him January 2005 when he first came to the Hill as the new incumbent senator of Illinois. I recall every detail of meeting and seeing him as if it happened just now. The first time I saw him, he was walking through the halls in the Capitol, and the first thing I noticed about him was his walk. My words, the man had swag out of this world. There was something in his walk that was different from what I had seen with most black men. Most black men have a distinctive walk, but there was something extraordinary in Mr. Obama's walk that was saying something profound in the stride in which he moved. There was quietness, eloquence, smoothness, power, and authoritativeness all in the same movements. Not only was his walk saying something, but he was as handsome and attractive as his walk. There was an aura so powerful it was like being in the presence of a thunderstorm with lighting flashing all around you. He exhibited power, strength, confidence, and authority. I sensed those things about him right away but couldn't recognize what it was that was resonating in him. Sometime later, I had the opportunity to meet him personally at a luncheon that was sometimes held by some of the senators for their constituents. I called Senator Obama's office and spoke to his administrative manager, Carolyn, and asked if they were planning a luncheon for his office, and if they were, when and where it would take place. I asked her to add my name and our legislative fellow Dr. Marlene Watson's name to the list for the luncheon, although neither of us was from Illinois. Our names were added, and the following week, the two of us attended the luncheon and met Senator Obama.

As we walked into the luncheon, he came over to us and extended his hand in a handshake, and there was something so powerful radiating from him that I knew couldn't be from anyone but God. My spirit bind witness to his spirit. I felt an anointing and knew instantly there was something beyond great about this man who would impact the world in some way. During our conversation, he talked to me and Marlene as if he had known us all our lives. He was personable and very genuine, and you knew and could feel that he had a heart for people.

After our conversation, I said to Dr. Watson that there was something extraordinary about Senator Obama and that he was sent there to turn things around. Three years later, when he announced his candidacy to run for president of the United States, it didn't surprise me. I thought, *Wow, what an impact he will have on this county and the world.*

When he made his announcement, I told Dr. Watson that he would win. I felt that so strongly in my spirit.

She said to me, "I hope you are right, but America is not ready for a black man to be President."

And I said to her, "No, America is not ready, but God is."

I said that because I believed with everything in me that what I saw and felt about this man was beyond man's control and God was doing a new thing for our country. I never once in all the time of his campaign spoke against or doubted that he would not become the leader of our nation because of what was revealed to me in my spirit when I met him.

When I would come back to Alabama on leave, I would tell people about Senator Obama. Many of them had never heard his name or knew who he was, and I thought how sad that was. But I had to remember this was Alabama, and unfortunately, many of my people I knew had no interest or had little interest at all about politics.

The night he won the election, after I did all my crying and celebrating at home alone, Dr. Watson was the first person I called. She had completed her fellowship with Senator Rockefeller's office and moved back to Pennsylvania to Drexel University, where she was on the staff. I had to call her because of what I told her did happen. She said to me when the announcement was made of him winning the election, I was the first person she thought of and knew that when her phone rang, it was me.

That night, she and I rejoiced and praised God together over the phone in celebration of our newly elected first African American president.

It was so rewarding to have witnessed this experience and live to see a black man become president of the United States, when at one time, our ancestors were salves to this country. I couldn't sleep that night after the election. There were so many things going through my mind—the idea that from the very continent that our ancestors were taken from, beaten, and brought to America as slaves had the bloodline and seed of one of us who would one day live in the White House and hold the highest honor and position that any man in this country could ever hold and become the president of the United States.

When I think about how I spent my days of picking and chopping cotton and how, thirty years later, I would be in a position to work in the very place where laws supporting slavery were imposed and put into place, it is profound.

Since I began writing my stories, I was fortunate enough to have visited the motherland. I visited Johannesburg, Soweto, and Cape Town in South Africa. I left my name in print at Johannesburg, South Africa. Winnie Mandela, the former wife of Nelson Mandela, had just passed during my visit there.

Jacob, our tour guide, took us to the home that Winnie and Nelson Mandela shared when they were married. When a person dies and you go to their memorial ceremony, there is a guest registration book at the entry of the door for guests to sign so you can let the family know who stopped by to pay their respects. I signed the guest book of Winnie Mandela, and I wrote these words: "Your struggles and legacy forever live throughout the world, and your name will forever be upon the lips of our people throughout eternity," signed Shirley Adkins, United States of America. I left my name, footprints, tears, and prayers in the continent where my ancestors originated from.

I was in South Africa for two and a half weeks, and each day was insightful and a blessing. As we were leaving for the airport to return to the US, my cousin Norma, and the four ladies I was traveling with, gathered in a circle, held hands, and prayed. There wasn't a dry eye among us after praying. I thanked God for allowing me to see more of His glory and creation in the place where my ancestors originated from.

It is my prayer that God will bless Africa with rain. As we first arrived in Johannesburg, the flight attendant welcomed us to South Africa, thanked us for flying with their airline, and then proceeded to tell us about the shortage of water. She asked if we would be sensitive to the amount of water we use due to the shortage of water from the lack of rain. Since returning to America, I have been sensitive to the water I use. Americans, as a whole, are very wasteful, and I am conscious now of leaving water running while doing dishes or when showering. I used to turn the water on and let it run for a while before getting into the shower, and since my visit to Africa, I have learned to appreciate the use and lack of water.

Africa is a beautiful continent. Every place I have been blessed to look upon, I see beauty. Beauty is seen through the mind and not only the eyes because everything God made is beautiful. People separate themselves in thinking that some places and people are better and different from others when in essence it's all the same everywhere, no matter what part of the world you travel or live in.

Barbara Ford, my first cousin, had a genealogical DNA test done for our bloodline. Barbara's mother and my mother were sisters. In this research, we discovered that our family is of Nigerian descent. I plan to go back to Africa one day, and Nigeria is where I will visit.

South Africa is beautiful in spite of the poverty and the negative things we see on television. Just like all places in this world, every country, continent, city, state, or nation has its place of wealth, beauty, and poverty. Wherever you go in life, prejudice, racism, poverty and wealth, and trials and tribulations are there. After this life, there is a greater reward waiting for us. It is when we leave this world and stand before God and answer for all that we have done. Each will receive whatever they deserve for the good or evil they have done in this earthly body (2 Corinthians 5:10).

As a race—Negro, black, colored, African American, or whatever your preference is to be called—our nationality alone is a story within itself because of our struggles. We all are a part of history, and we all have a story. My life is my story from the cotton fields to Capitol Hill. What's your story?

About the Author

Shirley Noel Adkins is a native of Alabama and a retiree from the legislative government in Washington, DC, where she served twenty-two years in the US Senate on Capitol Hill. Shirley attended Maple Springs Bible College and studied theology at Howard University's Saturday Bible College. After completing three years of MIT training, she became a certified and licensed minister to teach and speak the gospel of Jesus Christ. In ministry, she held various positions: counseling troubled teens, marriages, abused and battered women, and teaching ministry classes to teens and adults.

She is a proud mother of one son, three grandchildren, and four great-grandchildren. The atlas that has directed her life's journey is found in the book of Psalm 32:8, which states, "I will instruct you and teach you in the way that you should go, and I will guide you with my eye."

CPSIA information can be obtained
at www.ICGtesting.com
Printed in the USA
BVHW030601101121
621194BV00002B/58